101 EPIC THINGS TO DO IN RETIREMENT

Dream Big, Live with Purpose, and Love Your Life After 60

S.J. THOMAS

101 Epic Things to Do in Retirement: Dream Big, Live with Purpose, and Love Your LIfe After 60

Copyright © 2025 by S.J. Thomas and Sweet Harmony Press

All rights reserved. No part of this publication may be reproduced, distributed, or transmitted in any form or by any means, including photocopying, recording, or other electronic or mechanical methods, without the prior written permission of the publisher, except in the case of brief quotations embodied in critical reviews and certain other noncommercial uses permitted by copyright law. For permission requests, write to the publisher at the address below.

Sweet Harmony Press   info@sweetharmonypress.com

Ordering Information:

Quantity sales. Special discounts are available on quantity purchases by corporations, associations, and others. For details, contact the publisher at the address above.

Paperback ISBN: 978-1-948713-58-0

Ebook ISBN: 978-1-948713-59-7

Hardcover ISBN: 978-1-948713-60-3

Disclaimer:

This book is for entertainment and informational purposes only.

Sweet Harmony Press

2025

Join our email list to get all the latest news and book announcements.

If you enjoy this book, please consider leaving a review on amazon.com.

FIND YOUR WHY IN RETIREMENT

A Quick-Start Guide to Finding Purpose and Meaning in Your Retirement

What Sets Your Soul On Fire?

For decades, your purpose was built into the structure of your life – career goals drove your weekdays, family needs shaped your weekends, and the calendar told you where to be and when. Retirement changes everything. Suddenly you're facing a beautiful, terrifying abundance of choice: you can do anything, go anywhere, become anyone. But without a clear sense of why you're doing what you're doing, all that freedom can start to feel surprisingly empty.

Here's the hidden truth about retirement: without purpose, those golden years can quickly turn dark. Research shows that retirees lacking a sense of meaning face significantly higher rates of depression, social isolation, and declining health. The extended vacation feeling of early retirement fades fast, and what's left can feel surprisingly empty.

But there is good news: studies consistently show that retirees with a strong sense of purpose live longer, stay healthier, maintain sharper cognitive function, and report significantly higher life satisfaction. They're not just avoiding the negative outcomes—they're thriving in ways that working people often can't. And unlike your career years, when purpose was largely dictated by bosses, clients, and obligations, now you finally get to choose yours deliberately and authentically.

Finding Your Path Forward

"But I have so many interests!" or "My entire life has been my job and my family—where do I even start to find my Why?"

It can seem overwheming when there are so many choices before you. But it doesn't have to be. Your purpose isn't hiding in some distant, undiscovered corner of yourself—it's woven through your life experiences, revealed in the activities that energize you, visible in the problems that frustrate you, and reflected in the compliments people give you.

Your Six-Step Path to Purpose

The six steps that follow provide a systematic way to identify these patterns. Think of them as archaeological tools that help you excavate your purpose from the life you've already lived. Whether you have too many interests or feel like you have none, these exercises will help you:

- Recognize what truly matters to you versus what you think should matter
- Identify your natural strengths and how they can serve others
- Test potential purposes without making permanent commitments
- Build purpose into your daily life in practical, sustainable ways

You don't need to complete every exercise or answer every question. Start with the steps that intrigue you most, and let your curiosity guide you. Some retirees find their purpose in the first reflection exercise; others need to run several experiments before clarity emerges. Both paths are perfectly valid.

The goal isn't to have your entire retirement purpose figured out by next Tuesday. It's to take the first steps toward a life that feels meaningful, energizing, and authentically yours.

Let's begin.

Step 1: Reflect on Your Life's Wisdom (The "Looking Back to Move Forward" Exercise)

What to do: Grab a notebook and spend time answering these powerful questions:

Time and Flow
- Describe a time when you completely lost track of time because you were so absorbed in what you were doing. What were you doing? What made it so engaging?
- What activities make you feel most "in the zone" or fully present?
- When do you feel most like yourself?

Problems and Passion
- What issue in your community or the world makes you want to stand up and do something about it?
- If you could wave a magic wand and fix one problem in society, what would it be? Why does this matter so deeply to you?
- What injustice or inefficiency frustrates you most when you encounter it?

Freedom and Choice
- If money were no object and you had no obligations to anyone, how would you spend your days?
- What would you do even if no one paid you or thanked you for it?
- If you had unlimited resources and guaranteed success, what would you create or build?

Recognition and Strengths
- What do people consistently compliment you on or ask for your help with?
- What skills or knowledge do you have that friends and family regularly seek out?
- Complete this sentence: "People always tell me I'm good at..."

Peak Experiences
- Think of the three happiest or most fulfilling periods of your life. What were you doing? Who were you with? What made these times special?
- When have you felt most proud of yourself? What were you accomplishing?
- Describe a moment when you felt like you were making a real difference. What were the circumstances?

Legacy and Impact
- What knowledge or skills do you possess that would be a shame to take to the grave?
- If you could teach one thing to the next generation, what would it be?
- What problem in your community could you uniquely help solve?

Why this works: Your life experiences have already shown you what brings meaning. You're not discovering purpose from scratch – you're uncovering patterns that have always been there.

Time needed: Set aside 2-3 hours for deep reflection. Do this somewhere quiet where you won't be interrupted.

Step 2: Take the "Regret Test"

What to do: Imagine yourself at age 95 looking back on your retirement years. Write down what you would regret NOT having done, tried, learned, or contributed. Then ask yourself:

Relationships
- At age 95, which relationships would you regret not having invested more time and energy into?
- Who do you wish you had gotten to know better? What's stopping you now?
- What would you regret not saying to the people you love?

Experiences
- What adventures or experiences would you regret never having tried?
- What places would you wish you had visited?
- What skills or hobbies would you regret never learning?

Contribution
- What would you regret not having given back to your community?
- What cause or organization would you wish you had supported more?
- How would you regret not using your talents or resources to help others?

Growth and Learning
- What would you regret not knowing more about?
- What personal growth challenge would you wish you had tackled?
- What fear would you regret not facing?

Turning Regrets into Purpose
- Looking at your answers above, what patterns do you notice?
- Rewrite your top three regrets as positive purpose statements. (Example: "I'd regret not learning Spanish" becomes "Part of my purpose is connecting with other cultures through language")
- Which of these purpose statements excites you most? Why?

Why this works: Regret minimization is a powerful decision-making tool. The things you'd regret not doing reveal what truly matters to you beneath all the noise and "shoulds."

Action step: Turn each regret into a positive purpose statement. "I'd regret not traveling" becomes "My purpose includes experiencing diverse cultures." "I'd regret not helping struggling students" becomes "My purpose includes educational mentorship."

Step 3: Run the "Energy Audit"

Daily Tracking (Use these prompts each day for two weeks)

Morning: What activities do I have planned today?

Evening Reflection:
Which activities today gave me energy? (Rate each +2 to -2)
Which activities today felt meaningful? (Rate each +2 to -2)
What surprised me about my energy levels today?
What activity would I happily do again tomorrow?
What activity would I prefer to avoid or delegate?

Weekly Summary
- Which activities consistently scored high on both energy and meaning?
- Which activities drained my energy even though I thought I "should" enjoy them?
- What activities felt meaningful but exhausting? (These might need better boundaries or scheduling)
- What activities felt energizing but meaningless? (These are pleasant distractions, not purpose)
- Based on this week's data, what changes should I make to how I spend my time?

Pattern Recognition
- At what time of day do I feel most energized?
- Do I prefer working alone or with others?
- Do I gain energy from creative work, physical activity, helping others, learning, or building things?
- What common thread connects my high-scoring activities?

Why this works: Your body and emotions already know what gives you purpose – you just need to listen. Activities that score high on both energy and meaning are pointing toward your purpose. Activities that score low are stealing time from purposeful living.

Key insight: Purpose isn't always relaxing or easy, but it energizes you even when it's challenging. Notice which difficult activities still leave you feeling fulfilled versus which easy activities leave you feeling empty.

Step 4: Try the "Three Circles" Discovery Method

What to do: Draw three overlapping circles and label them:
Circle 1: "What I Love" (Your passions and interests)
Circle 2: "What I'm Good At" (Your skills and strengths)
Circle 3: "What the World Needs" (Problems you can solve, people you can help)

Your purpose lives in the center where all three circles overlap.

List items in each circle, then look for connections. Maybe you love gardening, you're good at teaching, and your community needs food security education – boom, there's a purpose direction.

Here are some prompts to help with this exercise.

Circle 1: What I Love (Your passions and interests)
- What topics could you read about or discuss for hours without getting bored?
- What activities make you smile just thinking about them?
- If you had a free Saturday with no obligations, what would you choose to do?
- What did you love doing as a child that you've lost touch with?
- What makes you feel most alive?
- When do you feel joy?

Circle 2: What I'm Good At (Your skills and strengths)
- What skills have you developed over your lifetime (both professional and personal)?
- What comes naturally to you that others find difficult?
- What do people regularly ask you to help them with?
- What awards, recognition, or achievements are you most proud of?
- What problems can you solve more easily than most people?
- What talents or abilities do you sometimes take for granted because they're so natural to you?

Circle 3: What the World Needs (Problems you can solve, people you can help)
- What problems do you see in your community that need solving?
- What groups of people need more support or advocacy?
- What causes or issues keep you up at night?
- If you could improve one thing about your neighborhood, what would it be?
- What resources, knowledge, or services are lacking in your area?
- What breaks your heart when you think about it?

Finding the Overlap
- Looking at your three circles, what items appear in multiple circles?
- Where do you see potential connections between what you love, what you're good at, and what's needed?
- Describe one possible purpose direction that combines elements from all three circles.
- How could you test this direction with a small experiment?

Why this works: Sustainable purpose requires all three elements. Passion without skill leads to frustration. Skill without passion feels empty. Neither matters if it doesn't serve others.

Step 5: Start Small with "Purpose Experiments"

What to do: Instead of declaring a grand purpose, run small experiments:
- Volunteer for one month at an organization aligned with your interests
- Take a single class in something that intrigues you
- Join one club or group related to a potential purpose area
- Commit to helping one person develop a skill you possess
- Spend one weekend working on a community project

Here are some steps to help with this step.

Before the Experiment
- What purpose direction am I testing with this experiment?
- What specific activity will I try?
- What do I hope to learn from this experiment?
- How will I know if this resonates with me?
- What concerns or hesitations do I have?

During the Experiment (Weekly Check-ins)
- What surprised me this week?
- What energized me?
- What felt harder than expected?
- What did I learn about myself?
- Am I looking forward to continuing?

After the Experiment (30-day Review)
- Did this activity align with what I love? How?
- Did it use my skills and strengths? Which ones?
- Did it address a real need? Whose need did it serve?
- What did I enjoy most about this experience?
- What would I do differently if I continued?
- On a scale of 1-10, how much does this feel like "my thing"?
- Do I want to expand this experiment, modify it, or try something completely different?

Why this works: You don't find purpose by thinking about it – you discover it by doing things and noticing what resonates. Small experiments let you test possibilities without major commitments while gathering real data about what fulfills you.

Critical rule: Give each experiment fair time (at least 30 days) before judging. Initial discomfort doesn't mean it's wrong for you.

Step 6: Connect Purpose to Daily Life (The Bridge Step)

Creating Your Purpose Appointments
- Based on my experiments and reflections, what purpose direction(s) feel most compelling?
- What specific activities align with this purpose?
- How many hours per week can I realistically commit to purpose-aligned activities?
- What days and times work best for my "purpose appointments"?
- What obstacles might interfere with these appointments? How can I address them?

Weekly Purpose Review
- Did I honor my purpose appointments this week? If not, what got in the way?
- How did I feel after engaging in purpose-aligned activities?
- What impact did I see from my efforts?
- What adjustments do I need to make for next week?
- Am I finding the right balance, or do I need to scale up or down?

Monthly Purpose Reflection
- How has my understanding of my purpose evolved this month?
- What activities are consistently fulfilling?
- What activities seemed good in theory but don't work for me?
- Who have I connected with through my purpose work?
- What have I learned or accomplished?
- What excites me about next month?

Ongoing Purpose Journal Prompts

Quarterly Deep Dive
- How has my sense of purpose deepened or changed this quarter?
- What activities am I ready to commit to long-term?
- What experiments should I let go of?
- How is my purpose affecting other areas of my life?
- What new purpose directions am I curious about exploring?

Annual Purpose Review
- How would I describe my purpose now compared to a year ago?
- What impact have I made this year?
- What brought me the most fulfillment?
- How has living with purpose changed me?
- What do I want to explore or deepen in the coming year?

When You Feel Lost
- When did I last feel deeply aligned with my purpose?
- What's changed since then?
- Am I trying to live someone else's purpose instead of my own?
- What would bring me back to center?
- What small step could I take today to reconnect with meaning?

Now that you have some clarity on your path, let's explore the possibilities that await you in your Epic Retirement!

COMMUNITY PROJECTS

#1 Create a Little Free Library Network

Create a Book Lover's Paradise in Your Neighborhood

A Little Free Library network is a collection of weatherproof book exchanges placed throughout your community. Each miniature library operates on "take a book, share a book," creating reading opportunities and connecting neighbors through shared stories. Your network removes barriers to reading while creating delightful discovery moments, turning dog walks and neighborhood strolls into treasure hunts for book lovers.

Getting Started

Map Your Territory: Identify high-traffic locations like parks, bus stops, walking paths, and friendly front yards. Look for spots where people naturally pause and have time to browse.

Design Your Libraries: Build simple weatherproof boxes or purchase ready-made units. Each needs a clear front, secure closure, and drainage. Make them distinctive and charming – these become neighborhood landmarks.

Recruit Host Locations: Approach homeowners, businesses, schools, and community centers about hosting libraries. Most people love the idea of promoting literacy in their neighborhood.

Stock with Variety: Include books for all ages and interests – novels, children's books, cookbooks, self-help, and local interest materials. Rotate stock regularly to maintain freshness.

Create Simple Guidelines: Post clear "take a book, share a book" instructions and basic care guidelines. Consider adding weather protection like plastic bags for rainy days.

Build Community Connections: Create a simple map or social media group to help people find all locations. Organize book drives and coordinate with local book clubs.

Maintain Your Network: Visit libraries regularly to tidy up, restock, and ensure they're in good condition.

The Sweet Rewards

You'll promote literacy throughout your community, create magical discovery moments for readers of all ages, build connections between neighbors, and become known as the person who made books accessible to everyone!

BUDGET: $300-$1,500 | TIME: 5-10 HRS/WEEK | DIFFICULTY: BEGINNER

#2 Start a Community Art Project

Turn Boring Walls into Beautiful Masterpieces

Starting a community art project brings people together, celebrates local culture, and creates something beautiful that everyone can take pride in. Public art transforms forgettable spaces into memorable ones, builds community pride, and often becomes beloved landmarks. Art makes neighborhoods more welcoming and valuable.

Getting Started

Choose Your Canvas: Scout for prominent walls, empty lots, or underutilized spaces. Think building sides, utility boxes, fence panels, or park areas that could use visual interest.

Get Official Approval: Contact property owners, city planning departments, and any relevant authorities. Most communities welcome beautification projects, but proper permits prevent problems later.

Rally Your Artists: Connect with local art teachers, retired artists, talented neighbors, and enthusiastic volunteers. You don't need Michelangelo – you need people who care about community.

Design Collaboratively: Host community meetings to gather input on themes, styles, and content. The best projects reflect local character and involve resident voices.

Plan Your Logistics: Organize supplies, weather considerations, safety equipment, and work schedules. Consider breaking large projects into phases manageable by volunteer schedules.

Document the Process: Take photos throughout creation – the community working together is often as beautiful as the finished art.

Celebrate Your Unveiling: Host a community celebration when completed. Make it a party that brings neighbors together to admire their collective achievement.

The Sweet Rewards

You'll beautify your community permanently, bring diverse neighbors together through shared creativity, potentially increase property values, and become known as the person who made your neighborhood more wonderful!

BUDGET: $500-$5,000 | TIME: 15-30 HRS/WEEK | DIFFICULTY: INTERMEDIATE

#3 Host a Senior-to-Youth Mentorship Program

Bridge the Generation Gap And Open Opportunities for Young and Old

A senior-to-youth mentorship program pairs experienced adults with young people seeking guidance, creating relationships that transfer knowledge while building mutual understanding. Young people crave authentic adult connections beyond what parents and teachers provide. Meanwhile, seniors have decades of wisdom, professional experience, and life lessons that shouldn't disappear. Your program creates bridges where both sides benefit enormously.

Getting Started

Partner with Organizations: Connect with schools, youth programs, community centers, or religious organizations that serve young people. Many already want mentorship programs but lack coordination.

Define Your Focus: Will you mentor on career guidance, life skills, specific hobbies, or general life wisdom? Having clear goals helps match mentors and mentees effectively.

Recruit Thoughtful Mentors: Look for patient, encouraging seniors who genuinely enjoy young people. Previous experience with kids helps, but willingness to listen matters more.

Screen and Train: Establish basic background checks and orientation sessions covering boundaries, communication styles, and program expectations. Safety first, meaningful connections second.

Create Structured Activities: Plan regular meeting formats – maybe monthly coffee chats, skill-sharing sessions, or project-based collaborations. Structure helps nervous participants feel comfortable.

Monitor and Support: Check in regularly with both mentors and mentees. Provide ongoing guidance and troubleshoot any relationship challenges that arise.

Celebrate Successes: Host events where pairs can share their experiences and accomplishments. Recognition motivates continued participation.

The Sweet Rewards

You'll help young people navigate life challenges, preserve valuable knowledge and skills, build meaningful intergenerational friendships, and discover that today's youth are pretty amazing when given proper attention and respect!

BUDGET: $200-$1,000 | TIME: 8-15 HRS /WEEK | DIFFICULTY: INTERMEDIATE

#4 Create a Community Repair Café

Turn "Throw It Away" into "Fix It Here" (And Keep Things Out of the Landfill)

A community repair café is a regular gathering where volunteer fixers help neighbors repair household items, electronics, clothing, and small appliances. Your repair café saves money, reduces waste, preserves repair skills, and builds community connections. Plus, there's something deeply satisfying about bringing dead things back to life.

Getting Started

Recruit Your Fix-It Squad: Find people who love tinkering – retired mechanics, seamstresses, electronics hobbyists, and anyone who enjoys problem-solving. You need various skills for different repair types.

Find Your Workshop Space: Scout community centers, libraries, church halls, or maker spaces with tables, good lighting, and electrical outlets. Storage for tools is helpful but not essential.

Gather Essential Tools: Start with basic repair tools – screwdrivers, pliers, sewing supplies, electrical testers, and cleaning materials. Many volunteers will bring their own specialized tools.

Set Your Schedule: Monthly weekend events work well, giving people time to gather broken items and plan attendance. Three-hour sessions allow time for complex repairs.

Create Simple Systems: Develop intake procedures, safety guidelines, and realistic expectations. Some items can't be saved, but the attempt often teaches valuable lessons.

Spread the Word: Advertise through community boards, social media, and local environmental groups. Emphasize the environmental benefits and community spirit.

Celebrate Successes: Document amazing saves, share before-and-after photos, and celebrate both successful repairs and learning experiences.

The Sweet Rewards

You'll reduce community waste, preserve valuable repair skills, save neighbors money, and create lasting friendships over shared problem-solving. Plus, you'll become the neighborhood hero who proves that "broken" doesn't have to mean "thrown away"!

BUDGET: $300–$1,500 | TIME: 8-15 HRS/WEEK | DIFFICULTY: INTERMEDIATE

#5 Start a Local History Preservation Project

Become Your Town's Memory Keeper (Before the Stories Disappear Forever)

A local history preservation project documents, organizes, and shares your community's past through photographs, interviews, documents, and artifacts. Every place has stor ies – families who built it, businesses that thrived and failed, events that shaped character, and ordinary people who lived extraordinary moments. These stories create identity and connection, but disappear quickly when storytellers age and physical evidence gets discarded.

Getting Started

Connect with Local Resources: Visit libraries, historical societies, museums, and city halls to understand what already exists and identify gaps in documentation.
Interview the Storytellers: Find longtime residents, business owners, and family descendants willing to share memories. Bring a simple recording device and prepared questions, but let conversations flow naturally.

Hunt for Visual Treasures: Collect old photographs, postcards, maps, newspaper clippings, and documents. Many families have shoeboxes of community gold they'd love to share.

Organize Systematically: Create digital archives with proper dating, labeling, and cross-referencing. Use simple database software or cloud storage that others can access and contribute to.

Share Your Discoveries: Create displays for libraries or community centers, develop walking tours, write articles for local papers, or build simple websites showcasing findings.

Engage the Community: Host "memory sharing" events where people bring artifacts and stories. Often one person's tale triggers others' recollections.

The Sweet Rewards

You'll preserve irreplaceable community heritage, uncover fascinating local secrets, build connections across generations, and become the go-to expert on local lore. Plus, you may uncover secrets that make your quiet town feel like the setting of a bestselling novel!

BUDGET: $500-$2,500 | TIME: 10-20 HRS/WEEK | DIFFICULTY: INTERMEDIATE

#6 Create a Community Seed Exchange

Turn Tiny Seeds into Giant Community Gardens

A community seed library and exchange is a free resource where neighbors share seeds, cuttings, and growing knowledge. People "check out" seeds in spring and "return" seeds from their harvest in fall. Your seed library preserves heirloom varieties, reduces gardening costs, builds local food security, and creates connections between gardeners.

Getting Started

Find Your Home Base: Partner with libraries, community centers, garden clubs, or cooperative extension offices. You need accessible space with cool, dry storage for seed packets.

Gather Founding Seeds: Collect donations from local gardeners, purchase heirloom varieties, and connect with seed companies that support community initiatives. Start with popular, easy-to-grow vegetables and flowers.

Create Simple Systems: Develop cataloging methods, storage solutions, and checkout procedures. Use envelopes, filing systems, and basic record-keeping to track what's available.

Host Seasonal Events: Organize spring "seed swaps" where people share varieties and growing tips, plus fall "harvest celebrations" where gardeners return seeds from successful crops.

Build Educational Components: Offer workshops on seed saving, starting seedlings, and preserving genetic diversity. Many gardeners want to learn these traditional skills.

Connect with Experts: Partner with master gardeners, agricultural extension agents, and experienced seed savers who can provide guidance and credibility.

Expand Thoughtfully: Add native plants, herbs, flowers, and unusual varieties based on community interest and local growing conditions.

The Sweet Rewards

You'll reduce neighborhood gardening costs, preserve heirloom varieties, build connections between gardeners, and create a more food-secure community. Plus, you'll become the go-to person for the best tomato varieties!

BUDGET: $200-$1,000 | TIME: 5-12 HRS/WEEK | DIFFICULTY: BEGINNER

#7 Start a Community Composting Initiative

Turn Your Neighborhood's Trash into Black Gold

A community composting program collects organic waste from neighbors and transforms it into nutrient-rich soil amendment. Food waste makes up about 30% of household garbage, and when it rots in landfills, it creates methane – a greenhouse gas that is nobody's friend. Your composting initiative diverts waste, creates valuable soil, and gives neighbors a reason to feel good about their banana habits. It's like being an alchemist, except instead of turning lead into gold, you're turning kitchen scraps into gardener's treasure.

Getting Started

Find Your Space: Look for community gardens, park areas, or even rotating backyard locations. You need space for compost bins and room for neighbors to drop off materials quickly and easily.

Get the Right Equipment: Invest in proper compost bins or build simple three-bin systems. You'll need basic tools (pitchforks, thermometers, wheelbarrows) and educational materials to help neighbors sort properly.

Educate Your Contributors: Host workshops on what can and cannot be composted. Pro tip: meat, dairy, and pet waste are the troublemakers that attract unwanted visitors and create unpleasant smells.

Create Collection Systems: Set up drop-off schedules, provide containers for households, and establish simple tracking to monitor how much waste you're diverting.

Plan Distribution: Decide how to share the finished compost – community garden use, neighborhood distribution, or fundraising sales to support the program.

The Sweet Rewards

You'll transform your neighbors into sustainability champions, create a local circular economy where waste becomes wealth, and become the neighborhood's go-to expert on turning trash into treasure.

BUDGET: $300-$1,500 | TIME: 5-10 HRS/WEEK | DIFFICULTY: BEGINNER

#8 Start an Animal Rescue Organization

Turn Your Empty Nest into a Haven for Furry (or Feathered) Souls

Starting an animal rescue is about creating second chances for animals in need, building a community of animal lovers, and discovering that your heart has infinite capacity for four-legged (or winged) family members. Every year, millions of animals end up in shelters through no fault of their own. Your rescue could be the bridge between "homeless" and "beloved family member."

Getting Started

Choose Your Mission: Will you focus on dogs, cats, exotic birds, reptiles, rabbits, or some other favorite animal? Consider your space, experience, and local need. Starting with one species keeps things manageable while you learn the ropes.

Get Legal and Legit: Register as a nonprofit, get proper licenses, and set up basic insurance. If you are considering being a wildlife rehabber, you will need specialized training. This sounds scary but most states have resources to help, and you'll need it for grants and donations.

Build Your Network: Connect with veterinarians, pet stores, and existing rescues. These relationships will become your lifeline for medical care, supplies, and adoption events.

Start Small, Dream Big: Begin with fostering through existing organizations to learn the process, then gradually take on your own rescue cases. Your first successful adoption will be addictive!

Create the Infrastructure: Set up intake procedures, adoption processes, and volunteer systems. It's like running a small business, except your "inventory" is warm and cuddly.

The Sweet Rewards

You'll save lives daily, connect families with perfect companions, build a network of amazing volunteers, and never lack for entertainment. Warning: You may become known as "the animal person" and find mysterious cats appearing in your yard!
Budget: $2,000-$15,000 startup | Time: 15-25 hrs/week | Difficulty: Intermediate

BUDGET: $2,000-$15K | TIME: 15-25 HRS/WEEK | DIFFICULTY: INTERMEDIATE

#9 Start a Community Garden

Ready to Turn Empty Lots into Grocery Stores?

A food desert is an area where fresh, affordable, nutritious food is hard to find. These areas lack full-service grocery stores, leaving residents relying on corner stores and fast food. Your community garden could be the oasis that changes everything! Starting a community garden in a food desert is about growing hope, community connections, and maybe the best tomatoes your neighbors have ever tasted.

Getting Started

Scout Your Territory: Look for vacant lots, unused park areas, or that weird patch behind the community center. If it's growing weeds, it can probably grow food!

Rally the Troops: Chat up neighbors and local organizations. You'll need 5-10 enthusiastic people who won't run when you start talking soil pH levels.

Navigate Red Tape: Contact city planning or property owners. Yes, there will be some paperwork. Yes, it feels like applying for a mortgage to grow carrots. But persistence will pay off!

Plan Out the Plot: Research which plants will grow well in your area, and design the garden for the best yields. Plan out the planting and harvesting schedule.

Fund Your Dream: Apply for grants, organize fundraisers, or crowdfund. Initial costs run $1,000-$5,000.

The Sweet Rewards

Beyond fresh vegetables, you'll create jobs, reduce food costs, build community connections, and become the local expert on everything from aphids to zucchini recipes.

BUDGET: $1,000-$5,000 | TIME: 10-15 HRS/WEEK | DIFFICULTY: INTERMEDIATE

#10 Create a Skill-Sharing Network

Turn Your Neighborhood into a Living University

A skill-sharing network connects people who want to learn with those who love to teach. Your neighborhood is full of incredible talent hiding in plain sight – retired engineers, master gardeners, expert cooks, and skilled craftspeople who've accumulated decades of knowledge. Your network becomes the bridge that connects these dots while building friendships and keeping everyone's minds sharp.

Getting Started

Map the Talent: Survey your community to discover who knows what. You'll be amazed – there's probably a retired chef, former engineer, master gardener, and quilting expert all within walking distance.

Find Your Hub: Set up base camp at a community center, library, senior center, or even rotating homes. You need space where people feel comfortable learning and teaching.

Create the Framework: Develop simple systems for matching teachers with students, scheduling sessions, and managing the network. Think potluck organization meets continuing education.

Launch Smart: Start with 3-4 popular skills (cooking, technology, crafts, home repair) and let word-of-mouth do the heavy lifting.

The Sweet Rewards

You'll witness beautiful intergenerational connections, discover hidden talents in your community, keep your own skills sharp by teaching others, and become the person who made learning fun again.

BUDGET: $200-$1,000 | TIME: 6-10 HRS/WEEK | DIFFICULTY: BEGINNER

#11 Establish a Scholarship Fund

Create a Lasting Legacy That Changes Lives

Your biggest financial worries are behind you, but for countless brilliant students, the dream of higher education hangs in the balance of tuition costs that seem to grow faster than weeds. Now you get to be the hero in someone else's "how am I going to pay for college?" story. Time to turn your nest egg into someone's launching pad! Your scholarship could be the difference between "I can't afford college" and "I'm going to be a doctor!" Plus, you'll get annual updates that are way more interesting than your investment portfolio reports.

Getting Started

Choose Your Focus: Decide what matters to you – local high school graduates, specific fields of study, financial need, or academic merit. Maybe you want to support future teachers, or kids who've overcome challenges, or budding entrepreneurs.

Pick Your Structure: Start small with $1,000-$5,000 annually, or go big with an endowed fund ($25,000+ that generates ongoing scholarships). You can work with your local community foundation, high schools, or colleges to manage the details.

Set the Criteria: Create clear guidelines for recipients. Make it meaningful but achievable – maybe they need to write an essay, maintain certain grades, or demonstrate community service.

Make It Official: Work with a nonprofit or foundation to handle the legal stuff. They'll manage applications, tax paperwork, and distribution while you focus on the fun part – picking winners!

The Sweet Rewards

You'll literally change lives, create lasting legacies, get invited to graduation ceremonies, and become the person families remember forever.

BUDGET: $1,000-$50,000+ | TIME: 5-8 HRS/WEEK | DIFFICULTY: INTERMEDIATE

#12 Start an Emergency Preparedness Program

Become Your Neighborhood's Superhero (Cape Optional)

An emergency preparedness program helps your neighborhood plan for natural disasters, power outages, or other unexpected events. Most people think emergency preparedness means buying extra batteries and hoping for the best. But real preparedness is about neighbors knowing neighbors, having communication plans, and creating systems that work when the power doesn't. It's like being a superhero, except instead of fighting villains, you're fighting panic with preparation and logic.

Getting Started

Rally Your Core Team: Find 4-5 neighbors who won't roll their eyes when you mention emergency kits. Look for the person who already has a generator and the one who knows everyone's business – both are valuable assets.

Assess Your Risks: Research what disasters are most likely in your area. Hurricanes? Earthquakes? Fires? Focus on realistic threats that need specific preparation.

Create the Plan: Develop communication trees, identify local resources, and establish meeting points. Make it simple enough that people will actually follow it when stressed.

Host Preparedness Events: Organize workshops on first aid, food storage, or emergency communications. Mix education with social time – think block party meets survival school.

Build Your Resources: Create neighborhood resource maps showing who has medical training, generators, or extra space. Encourage families to create emergency kits and communication plans.

The Sweet Rewards

You'll create a more resilient community, build lasting friendships, gain valuable leadership skills, and become the person everyone trusts in a crisis.

BUDGET: $500-$3,000 | TIME: 8-15 HRS/WEEK | DIFFICULTY: INTERMEDIATE

#13 Launch a Tool Library

Because Everyone Needs a Chainsaw Once Every Five Years

A tool library is exactly what it sounds like – a place where people can borrow tools instead of buying them. Think of it as Netflix for power tools, minus the binge-watching and plus the satisfying sound of things getting fixed! A tool library saves money, reduces waste, builds community connections, and turns you into the person everyone wants to know.

Getting Started

Find Your Space: Scout community centers, churches, unused garages, or basement spaces. You need secure storage and easy access – think library checkout vibes, not treasure hunt.

Start Small, Think Big: Begin with 10-20 essential tools (drills, saws, garden equipment). Scout garage sales for some cheap ways to get started. As word spreads, donations will pour in faster than you can organize them.

Create the System: Clearly label each tool as belonging to the library. Set up simple checkout procedures, maintenance schedules, and membership rules. Consider using library management software or even a simple spreadsheet to start. While the problem of theft will be a possibility, having the library list available for public viewing may be a way to keep people honest.

Spread the Word: Post on neighborhood apps, social media, and community boards. Host a "grand opening" with coffee and demonstrations.

The Sweet Rewards

You'll reduce neighborhood spending, create lasting friendships, learn about tools you never knew existed, and become the go-to person for "do you know where I can get...?" questions.

BUDGET: $500-$3,000 | TIME: 8-12 HRS/WEEK | DIFFICULTY: BEGINNER

#14 Start a Time Bank Bartering Service

Become the Neighborhood's Official Favor Exchange Coordinator

A time bank is a community exchange system where people trade services using time as currency. One hour of anyone's time equals one "time dollar," whether you're teaching piano or weeding gardens. It's like bartering, but with better bookkeeping and fewer arguments about what constitutes fair trade. Everyone has skills they enjoy using and tasks they'd rather avoid. Your time bank connects people who love organizing closets with those who need organizing help, while matching computer-savvy neighbors with folks who want digital photo tutorials. It builds community connections while getting things done.

Getting Started

Map Your Community's Talents: Survey neighbors about skills they'd love to share and services they need. You'll be amazed – there's probably a retired mechanic, master baker, and computer wizard all within walking distance.

Create Simple Systems: Use basic spreadsheets or time banking software to track exchanges. Members earn credits by providing services and spend them receiving help from others.

Start Small: Launch with 15-20 enthusiastic neighbors covering popular services like yard work, cooking, pet sitting, tutoring, or transportation.

Establish Guidelines: Set clear policies about safety, quality expectations, and dispute resolution. Most exchanges work beautifully, but having guidelines prevents awkwardness.

Host Regular Meetups: Organize monthly gatherings where members can connect, share success stories, and coordinate larger projects.

Expand Thoughtfully: Add new members gradually and consider specialized exchanges for different age groups or skill levels.

The Sweet Rewards

You'll strengthen community bonds, help neighbors discover hidden talents, create support networks that really work, and become the person who made everyone's life

BUDGET: $100-$500 | TIME: 5-10 HRS/WEEK | DIFFICULTY: BEGINNER

BUSINESS OPPORTUNITIES

#15 Invest in a Local Small Business

Become the Secret Weapon Behind Main Street's Next Success Story

Investing in local businesses means being part of something tangible while watching entrepreneurs' dreams come to life through your financial support, potentially earning recognition as a founding investor, and developing insider knowledge about the best local establishments that only comes from being actively involved in your community's economic development. You'll discover that local investing creates deeper satisfaction than abstract stock portfolios because you can see the direct impact on your community's economic health and build personal relationships with business owners who appreciate having local supporters.

Getting Started

Scout Your Targets: Look for established businesses seeking expansion capital or promising startups with solid business plans. Think beyond restaurants – consider service businesses, retail shops, or unique local concepts that fill real needs.

Do Your Homework: Review financial statements, understand their market, and assess the owner's experience and commitment. Don't invest more than you can afford to lose, but don't be so cautious that you miss great opportunities.

Structure the Deal: Work with a business attorney to create clear agreements. Will you be a silent investor, active partner, or advisory board member? Define expectations, profit-sharing, and exit strategies upfront.

Add Value Beyond Money: Share your network, offer strategic advice, and help with marketing or operations. Your experience in business, life, or specific industries could be worth more than your initial investment.

Stay Engaged: Attend regular meetings, celebrate milestones, and be available for guidance. The best investor relationships feel like partnerships, not just financial transactions.

The Sweet Rewards

You'll diversify your portfolio with potentially higher returns, build meaningful relationships, support your community's economic growth, and have fascinating stories about "your" businesses. Plus, you might just help create the next local institution!

BUDGET: $5,000-$100,000+ | TIME: 5-15 HRS/WEEK | DIFFICULTY: ADVANCED

#16 Start a Consulting Business

Turn Decades of "Been There, Done That" into "Pay Me for This Wisdom"

Starting a consulting business is about staying intellectually engaged, sharing valuable knowledge, and discovering that companies will pay surprisingly well for someone who actually knows what they're talking about. You have decades of accumulated knowledge that can't be Googled – industry relationships, crisis management skills, and the kind of institutional memory that prevents companies from repeating expensive mistakes. And you have something young consultants lack: the confidence to tell clients what they need to hear, not just what they want to hear.

Getting Started

Define Your Niche: Focus on your strongest expertise area – the thing people always asked your advice about. Whether it's marketing, operations, finance, or managing difficult personalities, specificity sells better than "general business advice."
Set Up Shop: Create a simple website, LinkedIn profile, and basic business structure. You don't need fancy offices – many successful consultants work from home offices (or coffee shops with good WiFi).

Price with Confidence: Research market rates and don't undervalue yourself. Your decades of experience command premium pricing. Start with project-based work to test the waters.

Network Strategically: Reconnect with former colleagues, join industry associations, and attend business events. Your existing network is your best source of initial clients.
Start Small, Scale Smart: Begin with one or two clients to refine your approach. Success in consulting often comes from referrals, so focus on delivering exceptional results rather than taking on too much too quickly.

The Sweet Rewards

You'll stay mentally sharp, earn meaningful income, build new professional relationships, and finally get paid what your advice is worth. Plus, you'll have the satisfaction of solving problems without dealing with office politics!

BUDGET: $500-$5,000 | TIME: 10-30 HRS/WEEK | DIFFICULTY: INTERMEDIATE

#17 Create and Sell a Product on Etsy

Create An Online Store That Is Uniquely You

Creating and selling products online is about validating your creativity, connecting with customers worldwide, and proving that age is just a number in the digital marketplace. The online marketplace is hungry for authentic, quality products made by people who actually care about craftsmanship. Your life experience gives you insights into what people really need, plus the patience and attention to detail that younger entrepreneurs often lack.

Getting Started

Identify Your Winner: Look at what you already make, fix, or create that people compliment or ask about. Could be woodworking, jewelry, organizational solutions, specialty foods, or digital products like patterns or guides.

Choose Your Platform: Etsy excels for handmade, vintage, and creative items. Amazon works better for practical products, books, or items you can produce at scale. Consider starting with one platform to learn the ropes.

Start Small, Test Smart: Create 5-10 items to test market response before investing heavily. Use your phone for initial product photos – good lighting matters more than expensive cameras.

Master the Basics: Learn about product descriptions, keywords, pricing strategies, and customer service. Most platforms offer free seller education resources.

Build Your Brand: Develop a consistent style, story, and customer experience. People buy from people they trust, and your authenticity is your competitive advantage.

Handle the Logistics: Set up simple systems for inventory, shipping, and taxes. Start basic and upgrade as you grow.

The Sweet Rewards

You'll turn hobbies into income streams, connect with customers who love your work, learn new digital skills, and maybe discover you're sitting on the next big thing. Plus, you'll have the best stories about unexpected international orders!

BUDGET: $200-$2,000 | TIME: 8-20 HRS/WEEK | DIFFICULTY: INTERMEDIATE

#18 Start a Food Truck or Mobile Business

Bring Your Favorite Foods Out To the World

A food truck or mobile business isn't just about slinging sandwiches (though those work great too). Think mobile coffee bars, tool sharpening services, pet grooming, or even a traveling bookstore. It's about taking what people need and bringing it where they are. A mobile business will have a low overhead compared to brick-and-mortar stores, built-in marketing appeal, and the flexibility to chase customers instead of waiting for them to find you.

Getting Started

Find Your Niche: What skill, service, or product could people use right where they are? Popular options include specialty foods, mobile repair services, pet care, retail products, or professional services like tax prep or notary work.

Research the Rules: Every city has different regulations for mobile businesses. Check permits, health department requirements, and zoning laws. Yes, it's paperwork, but it beats getting shut down on opening day.

Choose Your Wheels: Food trucks need commercial kitchens, but service businesses might work fine with a converted van or trailer. Consider buying used and retrofitting versus starting from scratch.

Plan Your Route Strategy: Scout locations, events, and regular stops. Think farmers markets, business districts during lunch, residential areas for services, or special events and festivals.

Master the Marketing: Social media is your best friend – post your location, daily specials, and behind-the-scenes content. Build a following of people who will chase you down for your amazing whatever-you-sell.

Start Small, Test Often: Begin with weekend markets or events before committing to full-time operation. Learn what works, what doesn't, and what customers really want.

The Sweet Rewards

You'll build a loyal customer base, enjoy ultimate flexibility, meet interesting people daily, and become a beloved part of your community's routine. Plus, you'll get paid to explore every corner of your area while bringing joy directly to people's doorsteps!

BUDGET: $15,000-$100,000 | TIME: 25-40 HRS/WEEK | DIFFICULTY: ADVANCED

#19 Launch a Bed & Breakfast or Airbnb

Turn Your Empty Rooms into a Hospitality Empire

Running a B&B or Airbnb transforms those quiet bedrooms into guest suites while meeting fascinating travelers from around the world, sharing your extensive local knowledge, and finally having the perfect excuse to invest in those luxurious towels you've always admired. This venture works perfectly for your life stage because you bring the experience to handle any guest situation with grace, the time to provide the kind of personalized service that creates five-star reviews, and probably a house that's actually clean and well-maintained now that the kids have moved out. Plus, you control your own schedule completely, taking breaks whenever you want while earning steady income from space that would otherwise sit empty.

Getting Started

Assess Your Space: Do you have spare bedrooms, a guest suite, or even a converted garage? Consider what makes your location special – proximity to attractions, peaceful setting, or unique character.

Research the Market: Check local regulations, HOA rules, and competitor pricing. Some areas require permits or have restrictions on short-term rentals.

Create the Experience: Focus on comfort, cleanliness, and thoughtful touches. Invest in quality linens, provide local recommendations, and create a welcoming atmosphere that reflects your personality.

Choose Your Platform: Airbnb works great for casual hosting, while traditional B&B marketing reaches people seeking more personal experiences. Consider starting with one platform and expanding.

Set Clear Boundaries: Decide on house rules, guest policies, and your availability. You're the host – set expectations that work for your lifestyle.

Master Guest Relations: Respond promptly to inquiries, provide clear instructions, and be available for questions. Great reviews lead to more bookings and higher rates.

The Sweet Rewards

You'll meet interesting people from around the world, earn steady income from unused space, become a local tourism expert, and have the best stories about unusual guest requests. Plus, you'll become an unofficial ambassador for your city, showing it off through locals' eyes!

BUDGET: $2,000-$15,000 | TIME: 10-25 HRS/WEEK | DIFFICULTY: INTERMEDIATE

#20 Create a Subscription Box Business

Become the Monthly Surprise Everyone Actually Wants

A subscription box business delivers carefully curated products to customers on a predictable monthly or quarterly schedule, creating anticipation and surprise with each delivery. Think of it as being a professional gift-giver who gets paid regularly for making people happy while discovering and sharing products they might never have found on their own. From artisanal foods and craft supplies to gardening tools and book collections, the possibilities are truly endless, limited only by your expertise and passion for specific niches or interests.

Getting Started

Find Your Passion Niche: What do you know better than anyone? Maybe it's regional foods, vintage finds, craft supplies, or wellness products. The more specific and passionate you are, the better.

Research Your Market: Check existing boxes, survey potential customers, and identify gaps. Is there really a need for another coffee box, or could you be the first to curate sustainable pet products?

Start Small and Test: Create a few sample boxes and get feedback from friends and online communities. Use this to refine your concept before investing heavily.

Source Your Products: Build relationships with small suppliers, artisans, and unique brands. Many vendors offer wholesale pricing for consistent orders.

Handle the Logistics: Set up subscription management software, packaging systems, and shipping processes. Start with monthly boxes to manage cash flow and workload. Build Your Community: Create social media presence, encourage unboxing photos, and engage with subscribers. The best boxes feel like joining a club, not just buying products.

The Sweet Rewards

You'll discover amazing products and makers, build a community of like-minded people, create anticipation and joy for hundreds of customers, and earn recurring revenue. Plus, you'll become a champion for small businesses and artisans who deserve more recognition!

BUDGET: $3,000-$20,000 | TIME: 15-30 HRS/WEEK | DIFFICULTY: INTERMEDIATE

#21 Start a Local Tour Guide Service

Turn Your "Back in My Day" Stories into Adventure Gold

Starting a tour guide service transforms your extensive local knowledge into captivating adventures while serving as your community's official ambassador, master storyteller, and the expert who reveals hidden gems that Google Maps will never discover. Your life experience and first-hand knowledge allows you to connect authentically with travelers of all ages, from curious families to fellow retirees seeking genuine local insights. Plus, you probably know incredible stories about your town's characters, forgotten events, and secret spots that even longtime residents have never heard about – the kind of insider knowledge that transforms ordinary sightseeing into unforgettable experiences that visitors treasure long after they return home.

Getting Started

Define Your Specialty: What makes your area unique? Historical walking tours, foodie adventures, ghost stories, architecture, nature walks, or behind-the-scenes access to local businesses? Focus on what genuinely excites you.

Research and Develop: Dig into local history, interview old-timers, visit museums, and discover stories even longtime residents don't know. The best tours combine well-known spots with surprising revelations.

Get Properly Licensed: Check local requirements for tour guide permits, business licenses, and insurance. Some areas require certification or testing – view it as professional credibility.

Create Your Routes: Plan 2-3 different tours of varying lengths and themes. Include bathroom breaks, photo opportunities, and places to rest. Test them with friends first.

Build Your Platform: Create simple marketing materials, join local tourism boards, partner with hotels and visitor centers, and establish an online presence. Word-of-mouth will be your best marketing.

Price Confidently: Research competitor rates and don't undervalue your expertise. Consider offering both group tours and private experiences at premium pricing.

The Sweet Rewards

You'll meet fascinating people from around the world, become a local celebrity, discover new things about your own town, and get paid for sharing stories you love telling anyway. Plus, you'll help people create memories that last long after they've returned home!

BUDGET: $500-$3,000 | TIME: 10-25 HRS/WEEK | DIFFICULTY: BEGINNER

#22 Launch a Pet-Sitting Business

Get Paid to Be Everyone's Favorite Neighbor (The One With Treats)

Starting a pet care business transforms your love of animals into meaningful service while providing invaluable peace of mind to busy pet parents who need someone reliable to care for their beloved family members. You'll become the trusted caregiver ensuring pets receive attention, exercise, and companionship when owners can't be there, all while getting therapeutic animal interaction that naturally reduces stress and boosts mood. This work keeps you active as you walk dogs, play with cats, and provide personalized attention that pets crave. You'll build genuine relationships with both animals and their grateful families while staying physically fit, emotionally fulfilled, and constantly entertained by the unique personalities of your four-legged clients.

Getting Started

Choose Your Services: Dog walking, pet sitting, overnight care, or specialized services like senior pet care? Consider your physical capabilities, schedule preferences, and which pets you connect with best.

Get Properly Insured: Invest in pet care liability insurance and bonding. It's not expensive, but it shows professionalism and protects you if Fluffy decides to redecorate someone's garden.

Build Your Reputation: Start with friends, neighbors, and referrals. Create profiles on pet care apps like Rover or Wag, but also develop your local network through word-of-mouth.

Set Clear Policies: Establish rates, cancellation policies, emergency procedures, and what services you do (and don't) provide. Being upfront prevents awkward conversations later.

Create Care Protocols: Develop systems for keys, feeding schedules, medication reminders, and daily updates. Pet parents love photos and progress reports!

Market Your Reliability: Emphasize your dependability, flexibility, and genuine love of animals. Many pet owners prefer mature, responsible caregivers over younger alternatives.

The Sweet Rewards

You'll get regular exercise, constant animal companionship, flexible scheduling, and the satisfaction of helping busy families. Plus, you'll have a job where every day brings

BUDGET: $200–$1,000 | TIME: 5–30 HRS/WEEK | DIFFICULTY: BEGINNER

#23 Create an Online Course

Transform Your Expertise into Passive Income Gold

Creating an online course transforms decades of hard-earned expertise into a global teaching platform while becoming the kind of instructor you wish you'd had – patient, practical, and genuinely invested in student success. You'll reach eager learners worldwide who are hungry for authentic instruction from someone who has actually lived through the challenges and developed real-world wisdom rather than just theoretical knowledge. You'll discover that people will gladly pay premium prices for clear instruction delivered by someone who can explain not just what to do, but why it works and how to avoid common pitfalls. Your courses become valuable resources that continue generating income while helping students achieve goals and creating a lasting legacy of knowledge transfer.

Getting Started

Identify Your Teaching Sweet Spot: What do people always ask you about? Could be professional skills, hobbies, life lessons, or practical knowledge. The best courses solve specific problems people actually have.

Choose Your Platform: Udemy and Teachable are beginner-friendly, while platforms like Thinkific offer more customization. Start simple – you can always upgrade later. Plan Your Curriculum: Break your knowledge into logical modules and lessons. Aim for 2-4 hours of content total for your first course. Quality matters more than quantity.

Create Your Content: Use basic screen recording software or your smartphone to film lessons. Good audio matters more than perfect video – invest in a decent microphone.

Add Value Beyond Videos: Include worksheets, templates, checklists, or bonus materials that make your course more valuable than free YouTube videos.

Price and Launch: Research similar courses for pricing guidance. Start conservatively and increase prices as you gain positive reviews and confidence.

Market Smart: Use your existing network, social media, and the platform's built-in audience. Students love courses from real practitioners, not just professional educators.

The Sweet Rewards

You'll create passive income streams, help people achieve their goals, build your reputation as an expert, and maybe discover you're a natural teacher. Plus, you'll prove that retirement can be your most productive and fulfilling chapter yet!

BUDGET: $100-$2,000 | TIME: 10-20 HRS/WEEK | DIFFICULTY: INTERMEDIATE

#24 Start an Antique Reselling Business

Turn Your "Junk" Radar into Cold Hard Cash

Starting a vintage reselling business transforms your eye for quality into a profitable treasure-hunting adventure while connecting exceptional items from the past with people who appreciate superior craftsmanship. You become a curator, rescuing well-made pieces from garage sale obscurity and giving them new life with collectors who understand their value. You'll develop expertise in recognizing authentic pieces while enjoying the thrill of discovery and matching special objects with people who will treasure them.

Getting Started

Develop Your Eye: Start by learning what's valuable in categories that interest you – furniture, jewelry, ceramics, books, or collectibles. Research completed sales on eBay and study price guides.

Choose Your Hunting Grounds: Estate sales, garage sales, thrift stores, online auctions, and storage unit sales all offer opportunities. Each requires different strategies and timing.

Pick Your Selling Channels: eBay for collectibles, Facebook Marketplace for furniture, specialized sites for specific items, or local antique malls for steady sales. Start with one platform and expand.

Create Your Workspace: Designate areas for cleaning, photographing, storing, and shipping items. Good photos make the difference between profit and loss in online sales.

Learn the Business Side: Understand sales tax requirements, keep detailed records, and factor in all costs including your time, storage, and shipping supplies.

Start Small and Learn: Begin with low-risk purchases to develop your skills. Every mistake teaches you something valuable about the market.

Build Your Reputation: Provide detailed descriptions, fast shipping, and excellent customer service. Positive reviews drive long-term success.

The Sweet Rewards

You'll combine treasure hunting with entrepreneurship, rescue beautiful items from neglect, meet fascinating sellers and buyers, and potentially discover items worth far more than you paid. Plus, you'll give forgotten heirlooms new life while connecting them with people who truly appreciate their value!

BUDGET: $500-$5,000 | TIME: 10-30 HRS/WEEK | DIFFICULTY: INTERMEDIATE

#25 Launch a Local Errand Service

Get Paid to Solve Problems and Help Busy Neighbors

A local delivery and errand service handles tasks busy people can't find time for – grocery shopping, prescription pickup, dry cleaning, waiting for repair services, or walking dogs. This service fills a genuine need where professionals, busy parents, and seniors struggle to manage routine tasks alongside other responsibilities. You become the problem-solver who makes people's lives run smoothly, handling everything from grocery runs to waiting for service appointments.

Getting Started

Define Your Services: Start with simple deliveries and pickups, then expand to grocery shopping, prescription runs, or waiting for service calls. Consider what tasks you actually enjoy doing.

Set Your Territory: Choose a manageable geographic area where you know the roads, businesses, and traffic patterns. Your local expertise is a huge selling point.

Price Your Time: Research competitors and factor in mileage, time, and convenience value. Don't undersell yourself – people pay premium prices for reliability and personal service.

Get Properly Insured: Update your auto insurance for business use and consider general liability coverage. It's not expensive but protects you and builds client confidence.

Create Simple Systems: Develop intake procedures, scheduling methods, and payment processing. Start with a simple phone and text system before investing in fancy apps.

Market Your Reliability: Emphasize your dependability, local knowledge, and personal touch. Many clients prefer working with established community members over faceless gig workers.

Build Gradually: Start with friends and neighbors, then expand through word-of-mouth. Regular weekly clients provide steady income and predictable schedules.

The Sweet Rewards

You'll become indispensable to busy families, seniors, and professionals while staying active and connected to your community. Plus, you'll discover that being genuinely helpful creates the most rewarding kind of work!

BUDGET: $200-$1,500 | TIME: 10-40 HRS/WEEK | DIFFICULTY: BEGINNER

#26 Create a YouTube Channel

Get Paid To Talk About Your Favorite Topics

Creating a monetized niche blog or YouTube channel transforms your deep knowledge into a thriving online business while building a loyal community around subjects you care about. Your decades of experience provide authentic expertise that younger content creators often lack, allowing you to provide genuine value to audiences hungry for real knowledge. This venture lets you share your wisdom while potentially generating income from something you'd enthusiastically discuss anyway.

Getting Started

Choose Your Perfect Niche: What could you talk about for hours without getting bored? Maybe it's antique restoration, regional cooking, gardening in specific climates, or local history. The more specific and passionate you are, the better.

Pick Your Platform: Blogs work great for detailed tutorials and written expertise, while YouTube excels for demonstrations and personality-driven content. Consider starting with whichever feels more natural.

Create Consistently: Start with one post or video weekly. Quality matters more than quantity, but consistency builds loyal audiences who eagerly await your next insight.

Focus on Helping People: Answer real questions your audience has. Share solutions to problems you've solved, mistakes you've learned from, and discoveries that excited you.

Build Your Community: Respond to comments, ask for feedback, and create content based on audience requests. Engagement matters more than follower counts.

Monetize Thoughtfully: Once you have regular viewers, explore affiliate marketing, sponsored content, digital products, or direct donations. Choose methods that feel authentic to your brand.

Stay Patient and Persistent: Building an audience takes time, but passionate expertise always finds its people.

The Sweet Rewards

You'll earn income sharing knowledge you love, build a global community of like-minded people, become a recognized expert in your field, and maybe discover you're a natural teacher!

BUDGET: $100-$1,000 | TIME: 5-15 HRS/WEEK | DIFFICULTY: ADV. BEGINNER

#27 Start a Microbrewery or Distillery

From Home Brewer to Local Legend

Starting a microbrewery or distillery transforms your passion for craft beverages into a legitimate business while creating a community gathering place where neighbors become friends over exceptional drinks. This venture combines your appreciation for quality craftsmanship with entrepreneurial ambition, turning a hobby into a local destination that showcases your dedication to creating something truly special.

Getting Started

Master Your Craft: Start with home brewing or distilling courses to perfect recipes and understand the science. Join local brewing clubs and visit established operations to learn from experienced makers.

Navigate the Legal Maze: Research federal, state, and local licensing requirements. Alcohol regulations are complex but manageable with proper guidance. Consider hiring a specialist attorney for setup.

Choose Your Focus: Will you specialize in beer, wine, spirits, or multiple beverages? Each requires different equipment, permits, and expertise. Starting narrow allows for quality focus.

Secure Your Location: Find suitable space with proper zoning, utilities, and room for production, storage, and potential tasting room. Consider industrial areas or agricultural zones.

Invest in Equipment: Quality fermentation vessels, bottling systems, and safety equipment are essential. Start with basic setups and upgrade as you grow.

Build Your Brand: Develop distinctive recipes, attractive packaging, and compelling story. Local ingredients and community connections create authentic marketing.

Plan Distribution: Decide whether to focus on on-site sales, local restaurants, or retail distribution. Each requires different business strategies and relationships.

The Sweet Rewards

You'll master an ancient craft, create a local business destination, potentially earn significant income, and become known as the person who makes the best drinks in town. Plus, you'll create a local institution that becomes part of your community's identity!

BUDGET: $50,000-$500,000+ | TIME: 40+ HRS/WEEK | DIFFICULTY: ADVANCED

#28 Launch a Specialty Farm

Turn Your Green Thumb into Green Dollars

A specialty farm focuses on high-value crops like gourmet herbs, exotic mushrooms, or specialty flowers rather than commodity crops. Think lavender for soap makers, shiitake mushrooms for restaurants, or heirloom herbs that make chefs weep with joy.

Getting Started

Choose Your Specialty: Research what's in demand locally – maybe microgreens for restaurants, medicinal herbs for wellness enthusiasts, or cut flowers for florists. Visit farmers markets to see what's missing.

Start Small and Smart: Begin with a few high-value crops in a manageable space. A greenhouse, basement setup, or even unused rooms can launch mushroom operations.

Master Your Craft: Take courses, read extensively, and connect with experienced growers. Each specialty has unique requirements for soil, climate, harvesting, and post-harvest handling.

Build Customer Relationships: Connect directly with restaurants, farmers markets, florists, or health food stores. Personal relationships create loyal customers who'll pay premium prices.

Invest in Quality Infrastructure: Proper growing facilities, irrigation systems, and post-harvest storage are crucial for specialty crops. Start basic but plan for expansion.

Perfect Your Timing: Learn seasonal demand patterns and plan production accordingly. Some crops need year-round availability while others are seasonal specialties.

Market Your Story: Customers love knowing their grower. Share your growing methods, passion for quality, and commitment to local food systems.

Scale Gradually: Add new crops, expand growing space, or increase production based on proven demand rather than hopeful projections.

The Sweet Rewards

You'll create a profitable business doing work you love, supply local markets with unique products, become known as the area's specialty crop expert, and maybe discover you're sitting on agricultural gold!

BUDGET: $2,000-$25,000 | TIME: 20-40 HRS/WEEK | DIFFICULTY: INTERMEDIATE

#29 Start a Petting Farm Animal Experience

Create a Magic Wonderland for Kids

A family-friendly petting farm creates magical hands-on experiences where visitors can feed, pet, and learn about gentle farm animals. This venture addresses a real need where many children have never touched a farm animal or understand how food reaches their table. Your petting farm becomes the bridge between urban life and agricultural reality, offering authentic experiences that create lasting memories.

Getting Started

Choose Your Animal Stars: Start with gentle, kid-friendly animals like miniature goats, sheep, rabbits, chickens, and maybe a gentle pig or two. Avoid animals that are unpredictable or require specialized care initially.

Prepare Your Space: Fence areas securely, create shaded spots, and ensure proper drainage. Animals need shelter, fresh water, and safe spaces away from visitors when needed.

Learn Animal Care: Take courses in livestock management, animal health, and safety protocols. Partner with local veterinarians for ongoing health care and emergency support.

Plan Your Experience: Create structured activities like feeding times, educational talks, and hands-on experiences. Consider seasonal events like baby animal visits in spring.

Handle Regulations: Research zoning requirements, insurance needs, and health department regulations. Many areas require permits for agritourism operations.

Build Safety Protocols: Develop clear rules for animal interactions, hand-washing stations, and emergency procedures. Safety first, fun second.

Market to Families: Connect with schools, daycare centers, birthday party planners, and family groups. Social media showcasing cute animals practically markets itself.

The Sweet Rewards

You'll create magical memories for countless children, educate families about agriculture, provide therapeutic animal interactions, and wake up every day surrounded by creatures that are genuinely happy to see you!

BUDGET: $5,000-$50,000 | TIME: 25-40 HRS/WEEK | DIFFICULTY: ADVANCED

ARTISTIC ENDEAVORS

#30 Write and Self-Publish a Book

Create Your Literary Legacy (And Become a Published Author)

Writing and publishing transforms your life experiences into lasting literary works while preserving your unique legacy for future generations. This creative journey allows you to process your life's adventures while potentially inspiring others who face similar challenges. Your writing becomes a bridge between your experiences and readers seeking wisdom or connection.

Getting Started

Choose Your Path: Memoir lets you share real experiences and family history, while fiction gives you creative freedom to explore "what if" scenarios. Both have audiences hungry for authentic voices.

Start Writing Daily: Set aside 30-60 minutes each day. Don't worry about perfection – just get stories down on paper. Many successful authors write just 250 words per day.

Join a Writing Group: Connect with local writers or online communities for support, feedback, and accountability. Other writers understand the journey and celebrate small victories.

Learn the Craft: Take online courses, read books about writing, or attend workshops. Storytelling basics can be learned at any age.

Embrace Technology: Use tools like Scrivener for organizing or dictation software if typing is challenging. Modern publishing is surprisingly accessible.

Plan Your Publishing: Amazon KDP and other platforms make self-publishing straightforward. You maintain control and keep higher royalties.

Build Your Platform: Start a simple blog, join social media, or speak at local groups. Readers love connecting with authors who have real stories to tell.

The Sweet Rewards

You'll preserve family history, potentially earn ongoing royalties, gain respect as a published author, and maybe discover you have more books in you than you thought. Plus, you'll create something permanent that your family will treasure for generations!

BUDGET: $500-$3,000 | TIME: 10-20 HRS/WEEK | DIFFICULTY: INTERMEDIATE

#31 Learn to Paint with Watercolors

From "I Can't Even Draw a Stick Figure" to Gallery Opening Night

Watercolor painting transforms simple pigment and water into a meditative practice that creates beautiful art while helping you discover hidden artistic talents. Watercolors are perfectly suited for beginners because they're forgiving, portable, and clean up easily. Those "happy accidents" that happen when pigments flow unexpectedly often create the most beautiful effects in your artwork.

Getting Started

Gather Your Supplies: Start with basic watercolor paints, brushes, and watercolor paper. Don't go expensive initially – you can upgrade as you develop skills.

Take a Class: Local art centers, community colleges, or online platforms offer beginner courses. Having a teacher prevents bad habits and provides encouragement.

Practice Daily: Even 30 minutes a day shows dramatic improvement. Start with simple subjects like fruits, flowers, or landscapes. YouTube tutorials offer free instruction.

Study the Masters: Visit galleries, check out library books, and analyze different watercolor styles. You'll develop your own preferences and techniques.

Document Your Progress: Keep all your paintings, even the "disasters." You'll be amazed at your improvement, and early attempts become charming memories.

Plan Your Exhibition: Contact local coffee shops, libraries, or small galleries about displaying your work. Many venues love featuring local artists.

Host Your Opening: Invite friends, family, and neighbors to celebrate your journey. Provide refreshments and tell the story behind each piece.

The Sweet Rewards

You'll develop a relaxing hobby that travels anywhere, create unique gifts for loved ones, potentially sell your artwork, and join a welcoming community of artists. Plus, you'll prove to yourself that creativity has no age limit – it only gets better with experience!

BUDGET: $200-$1,500 | TIME: 5-15 HRS/WEEK | DIFFICULTY: BEGINNER TO INT

#32 Start a Pottery Studio in Your Garage

Turn Your Car Storage into Clay Magic Central

Starting a pottery studio transforms your space into a sanctuary where you connect with one of humanity's most ancient crafts, discovering the deeply meditative rhythm of the spinning wheel and the satisfaction of shaping raw clay into functional art with your own hands. This venture allows you to slow down and focus completely on the present moment as you center clay and create vessels that blend beauty with utility, potentially becoming the go-to artist everyone asks to create custom wedding gifts and special occasion pieces. You'll join a tradition that spans millennia while developing your own unique style and discovering that working with clay provides a perfect balance of creative challenge and therapeutic calm.

Getting Started

Assess Your Space: Clear out that garage, basement, or spare room. You need good ventilation, water access, and space for a wheel, kiln, and storage.

Take Classes First: Learn the basics at a local pottery studio before investing in equipment. You'll discover preferences and avoid expensive mistakes.

Start with Essential Equipment: A pottery wheel, basic tools, clay, and glazes get you started. You can rent kiln time initially or buy a small kiln later.

Master the Fundamentals: Focus on centering clay, pulling walls, and basic forms before attempting fancy techniques. Even masters still practice basic bowls.

Experiment with Glazes: This is where the magic happens! Testing different glazes and firing techniques creates unique finishes.

Build Your Community: Connect with local potters, join ceramic guilds, and attend pottery shows. The pottery world is welcoming and generous with knowledge.

Share Your Creations: Start giving pieces as gifts, selling at markets, or teaching neighbors. Your garage studio could become the neighborhood's creative hub.

The Sweet Rewards

You'll join an ancient tradition of ceramic artists, create functional beauty that enhances daily life, develop remarkable dexterity and strength, and always have handmade gifts that show you truly care.

BUDGET: $1,500-$8,000 | TIME: 8-20 HRS/WEEK | DIFFICULTY: INTERMEDIATE

#33 Create a Documentary

Transform Your Community's Stories into Cinema Gold

Creating a documentary transforms filmmaking into a preservation mission, capturing important stories before they disappear and connecting generations through shared narratives. This endeavor allows you to become both historian and filmmaker, interviewing people whose memories hold keys to understanding how your community evolved while developing video production skills that turn ordinary conversations into compelling viewing experiences.

Getting Started

Choose Your Focus: Will you cover your town's founding, a specific era, local legends, or prominent families? Maybe focus on how a major event changed everything, or the stories behind familiar landmarks.

Research Like a Detective: Visit local libraries, historical societies, and newspaper archives. Talk to longtime residents, check city records, and hunt down old photographs.

Gather Your Equipment: A decent smartphone, basic tripod, and simple editing software get you started. Many libraries offer free video editing classes.

Interview the Storytellers: Find people who lived through important events or whose families passed down stories. Prepare questions but let conversations flow naturally.

Collect Visual Materials: Hunt for old photos, maps, postcards, and documents. Many families have treasure troves they'd love to share.

Learn Basic Editing: Free software like iMovie or DaVinci Resolve can create professional results. YouTube tutorials teach everything you need.

Plan Your Premiere: Contact your local library, community center, or historic society about hosting a screening. Make it a community event with popcorn and discussion.

The Sweet Rewards

You'll rescue vanishing memories from disappearing forever, develop expertise that makes you invaluable to researchers, forge meaningful relationships with community elders, and build a historical archive that enriches your area permanently. Plus, you'll ensure that remarkable people and events are never forgotten!

BUDGET: $200-$2,000 | TIME: 15-30 HRS/WEEK | DIFFICULTY: INTERMEDIATE

#34 Learn Creative Photography

Turn Your "Point and Shoot" into Professional Portfolio Magic

Learning photography transforms your relationship with the visual world, teaching you to see light, composition, and fleeting moments with an artist's eye. This creative pursuit becomes a way of preserving moments and places that matter to you, from family gatherings to natural landscapes. You'll discover that photography encourages you to slow down and find beauty in ordinary scenes.

Getting Started

Master Your Equipment: Whether it's a smartphone, point-and-shoot, or the latest DSLR, learn what it can really do. Take a photography class or watch online tutorials about composition and lighting.

Find Your Subject Matter: What draws your eye? Local architecture, nature, people, abstract patterns, or disappearing traditions. The best coffee table books have a clear theme.

Study Light and Timing: Learn about golden hour, blue hour, and how different light changes your subjects. Great photographers are students of light.

Practice Daily: Take photos every day, even around your house or neighborhood. Challenge yourself with different subjects, angles, and lighting conditions.

Learn Basic Editing: Simple photo editing software can transform good shots into great ones. Focus on enhancing what you captured rather than creating fantasy images.

Curate Your Best Work: Develop a critical eye for selecting your strongest images. A coffee table book needs 40-60 exceptional photos, not 400 okay ones.

Plan Your Book: Choose a theme, write compelling captions, and design layouts that let your images breathe. Online services make professional book printing affordable.

The Sweet Rewards

You'll become a visual historian of your own life and community, develop an artistic skill that improves with every shot, potentially build income streams from your creativity, and create gifts that people actually treasure.

BUDGET: $300-$3,000 | TIME: 8-20 HRS/WEEK | DIFFICULTY: INTERMEDIATE

#35 Start a Community Theater Group

Bring Broadway to Your Backyard

Starting a community theater group transforms your neighborhood into a creative hub while building meaningful connections between people who might never have spoken otherwise. This venture creates a supportive environment where people can step outside their comfort zones and surprise themselves with hidden talents, all while working toward memorable performances that bring joy to both participants and audiences.

Getting Started

Gather Your Cast: Start by finding 8-10 enthusiastic people who won't run when you mention "memorizing lines." Look for folks who love reading aloud, telling stories, or being the center of attention.

Find Your Stage: Scout community centers, libraries, church halls, or outdoor spaces. You don't need Broadway – just somewhere people can gather, project voices, and store props.

Choose Your First Production: Start with simple, well-known plays or crowd-pleasing musicals. Think "Our Town," short comedies, or reader's theater that doesn't require elaborate sets.

Build Your Support Crew: You'll need people who love being behind the scenes – set painters, costume creators, lighting operators. Many theater lovers prefer backstage to spotlight.

Plan Your Rehearsal Schedule: Meet weekly for 6-8 weeks before performance. Keep it fun and flexible – this is community theater, not professional auditions.

Create Your Audience: Market through local newspapers, social media, and word-of-mouth. Price tickets affordably and make it a community celebration.

Celebrate Your Opening Night: Host a cast party after your first show. You'll have created something magical together, and everyone will be asking "What's our next play?"

The Sweet Rewards

You'll discover hidden talents in your neighbors, create lasting friendships, bring joy to your community, and find your own inner performer. Every show becomes a celebration of what ordinary people can accomplish when they support each other's dreams!

BUDGET: $500-$3,000 | TIME: 10-20 HRS/WEEK | DIFFICULTY: INTERMEDIATE

#36 Learn to Play a Musical Instrument

From Air Guitar Hero to Actual Rock Star (Age Is Just a Number)

Time to fulfill that dream of learning to play music and discover the joy you've been missing! Playing an instrument and performing with others transforms you into a genuine music maker while building impressive cognitive strength that keeps your mind sharp, unlocking powerful new emotional outlets for feelings you might struggle to express in words, and revealing firsthand why musical connection feels so essential to human happiness. This musical journey provides mental stimulation that rivals any brain training program while connecting you to the universal language that transcends boundaries, creating bonds with fellow musicians that often become some of the most rewarding friendships of your retirement years.

Getting Started

Choose Your Weapon: Guitar, piano, drums, bass, ukulele, pan flute, bodhran or harmonica – pick something that genuinely excites you. Don't worry about what's "age-appropriate." If you want electric guitar, rock on!

Find Your Teacher: Look for instructors who work with adult beginners. Many music stores offer group classes that are both affordable and social.

Practice Smart: Set realistic goals – even 15-20 minutes daily beats marathon weekend sessions. Focus on songs you enjoy rather than just scales.

Connect with Musicians: Check community centers, music stores, and online groups for jam sessions. Many towns have groups specifically for amateur adult musicians.

Start Performing Early: Don't wait until you're "ready" – join open mic nights, play at family gatherings, or perform at coffee shops. Experience teaches more than solo practice.

Join or Form a Band: Look for enthusiastic amateurs who prioritize fun over perfection. Many communities have senior bands, classic rock groups, or casual jam bands.

The Sweet Rewards

You'll boost your cognitive function, gain a creative outlet for stress, make new friends who share your musical interests, and maybe even perform for appreciative audiences. You'll prove that it's never too late to become the musician you always dreamed of being!

BUDGET: $300-$2,000 | TIME: 5-10 HRS/WEEK | DIFFICULTY: BEGINNER TO INTER

#37 Create a Podcast Favorite Topics

Turn Your Wisdom into Amazing Audio Content

Creating a podcast transforms your voice into a powerful communication tool for building engaged communities around shared interests, establishing yourself as a trusted expert in subjects you care about. This medium allows you to share knowledge in an intimate, conversational format that creates authentic connections with listeners, while building a loyal audience that values your perspective.

Getting Started

Choose Your Niche: What could you talk about for hours without getting bored? Maybe it's local history, gardening tips, book reviews, cooking wisdom, travel stories, or life advice. The more specific and passionate you are, the better.

Start Simple with Equipment: A decent USB microphone, free recording software like GarageBand or Audacity, and a quiet room gets you started.

Plan Your Format: Will you do solo episodes, interview guests, or mix both? Start with 15-30 minute episodes – people's attention spans and your comfort level will thank you.

Record Your First Episodes: Batch record 3-4 episodes before launching so you have content ready. Don't aim for perfection – aim for authenticity and helpful information.

Build Your Audience Gradually: Share with friends and family first, then expand through social media, local groups, and online communities related to your topic.

Stay Consistent: Whether weekly, bi-weekly, or monthly, consistency builds loyal listeners better than sporadic bursts of multiple episodes.

Engage with Your Community: Respond to comments, ask for topic suggestions, and maybe even feature listener questions or stories.

The Sweet Rewards

You'll become a recognized expert in your passion area, meet fascinating people through interviews, build a global community of like-minded individuals, and maybe even monetize your knowledge while discovering your thoughts resonate with people unexpectedly!

BUDGET: $100-$1,000 | TIME: 3-8 HRS/WEEK | DIFFICULTY: BEGINNER

#38 Start a Quilting Circle for Charity Quilts

Turn Your Love of Quilting into Meaningful Community Service

Starting a charity quilting circle combines creativity with genuine compassion while turning weekly coffee chats into productive community service that makes a real difference in people's lives. This meaningful activity creates a perfect blend of social connection, artistic expression, and charitable giving that benefits both the makers and the recipients.

Getting Started

Gather Your Circle: Find 6-8 people who love crafts, socializing, or helping others. Quilting skills can be learned, but enthusiasm for community service is what matters.

Choose Your Beneficiary: Pick a local charity that needs quilts – animal shelters, homeless shelters, children's hospitals, or nursing homes. Having a specific cause gives your group purpose.

Establish Your Meeting Rhythm: Weekly or bi-weekly gatherings work best. Rotate hosting duties or find a consistent location like a community center or library.

Start Simple: Begin with basic patterns like strip quilts or simple squares, and work up into more complex designs.

Create Your Supply System: Pool resources for fabric, batting, and thread. Many members probably have fabric collections. Thrift stores become treasure hunts.

Develop Production Flow: Some people cut, others piece, others quilt. Playing to individual strengths makes the process efficient and enjoyable.

Plan Delivery Events: Make presenting finished quilts to your charity a group celebration. Seeing the joy your work brings makes every pricked finger worthwhile.

The Sweet Rewards

You'll master a beautiful traditional craft, build deep friendships through shared projects, provide comfort to those who need it most, and always have the perfect meaningful gift. Plus, you'll finally have a legitimate reason for your fabric obsession!

BUDGET: $200-$800 | TIME: 6-12 HRS/WEEK | DIFFICULTY: BEG. TO INTERMEDIATE

#39 Create a Sculpture Garden in Your Yard

Turn Your Lawn into an Outdoor Art Gallery

Creating a sculpture garden transforms your ordinary yard into a carefully curated outdoor art experience while providing valuable support to talented local artists who need platforms to showcase their work. You'll combine your appreciation for fine art with landscape design, creating flowing pathways that guide visitors through an ever-changing gallery where each season brings new perspectives.

Getting Started

Survey Your Canvas: Walk your property at different times of day and seasons. Notice how light changes, where natural gathering spots exist, and which areas need visual interest.

Define Your Vision: Will you focus on a specific style, material, or theme? Maybe contemporary metal pieces, stone carvings, or repurposed industrial art. Having a concept helps create cohesion.

Start with Pathways: Create routes that lead visitors naturally from piece to piece. Use existing walkways or add gravel paths, stepping stones, or mulched trails.

Mix Scales and Heights: Combine large statement pieces with smaller intimate works. Place some sculptures at eye level, others that make people look up or crouch down.

Support Local Artists: Connect with local art schools, studios, and emerging artists. Many would love the opportunity to show their work before they become expensive.

Consider the Seasons: Choose pieces that look good year-round or plan seasonal rotations. Some sculptures are enhanced by snow, others shine in summer gardens.

Add Lighting: Simple solar lights or low-voltage landscape lighting extends viewing hours and creates dramatic evening effects.

The Sweet Rewards

You'll create a unique outdoor space that brings joy year-round, support local artists, increase your property value, and become known as the interesting neighbor with amazing taste. Your garden will become a living gallery that evolves and grows more

BUDGET: $1,000-$15,000 | TIME: 5-15 HRS/WEEK | DIFFICULTY: INTERMEDIATE

#40 Start a Writers' Group

Turn Your Book Club into a Publishing House

Starting a writers' group and publishing an anthology transforms casual storytellers into legitimate published authors while fostering a supportive creative community that encourages artistic growth. This collaborative venture creates accountability that solo writing often lacks, while the shared goal of producing a published anthology gives everyone a concrete deadline and tangible reward.

Getting Started

Gather Your Literary Circle: Start with 6-8 people who love reading, storytelling, or good conversation. Don't worry about writing experience – enthusiasm matters more than published credentials.

Choose Your Meeting Format: Weekly or bi-weekly gatherings work best. Rotate hosting duties or find a consistent location like a library or community center.

Establish Ground Rules: Create guidelines for constructive criticism, reading time limits, and meeting structure. You're building confidence, not crushing dreams.

Start with Writing Prompts: Use simple exercises to get everyone comfortable sharing work. Try memoir pieces, short fiction, or poetry. The goal is to start writing.

Learn Together: Bring in guest speakers, attend writing workshops, or read craft books as a group. Many successful writers share knowledge with enthusiastic groups.

Develop Your Anthology Theme: Maybe local history, life lessons, travel adventures, or family stories. Having a unifying theme helps create a cohesive collection.

Plan Your Publication: Decide whether to self-publish through platforms like Amazon KDP or work with a local printer. Include photos and author bios.

The Sweet Rewards

You'll improve your writing skills, build lasting friendships through shared creativity, preserve important stories, and become published authors. Your journey from casual writers to published authors will prove that it's never too late to take creative dreams seriously!

BUDGET: $300-$2,000 | TIME: 5-10 HRS/WEEK | DIFFICULTY: BEG. TO INTERM.

#41 Build Heirloom Furniture

Turn Your Garage into a Master Craftsman's Workshop

Learning woodworking and building heirloom furniture transforms you into a skilled craftsperson connecting with ancient traditions while producing beautiful pieces that improve with time. This rewarding craft allows you to work with natural materials using time-tested techniques, creating functional art that provides your family with treasured pieces they'll pass down as meaningful heirlooms.

Getting Started

Set Up Your Workshop: Clear out that garage or basement and create a dedicated workspace. You need good lighting, ventilation, and room for larger pieces. Start with basic hand tools before power equipment.

Learn the Fundamentals: Take a local woodworking class or find an experienced mentor. Understanding wood grain, proper joinery, and finishing techniques prevents expensive mistakes.

Start with Simple Projects: Begin with cutting boards, small boxes, or simple shelves. Master basic techniques like measuring, cutting, and sanding before attempting furniture.

Choose Quality Materials: Invest in good hardwood lumber rather than construction-grade pine. Working with beautiful wood makes the process more enjoyable.

Master Hand Tools First: Learn to use chisels, hand planes, and measuring tools properly. Hand tool skills make you a better woodworker even with power tools.

Plan Your Heirloom Pieces: Design furniture that reflects your family's needs. Maybe a dining table for holidays, hope chest for grandchildren, or built-in bookcases.

Focus on Joinery: Learn traditional joints like dovetails, mortise and tenon. Strong joinery is what makes furniture last generations, not just glue and screws.

The Sweet Rewards

You'll develop a deeply satisfying skill, create lasting family treasures, save money on quality furniture, and always have the perfect gift for special occasions. Your handmade pieces will become family heirlooms that tell the story of your dedication to excellence and life-long learning!

BUDGET: $1,000-$5,000 | TIME: 10-25 HRS/WEEK | DIFFICULTY: INTERM. TO ADV.

#42 Create an Art Therapy Program

Become the Healing Hero with Paint Brushes and Good Vibes

Creating an art therapy program for seniors opens amazing possibilities for healing and connection. You'll use artistic creation as a gentle pathway to emotional wellness that often works better than traditional approaches, while building meaningful connections between participants through shared creativity and mutual support. Art becomes the bridge that helps people express feelings they struggle to put into words. You'll watch seniors discover new ways to process life experiences through painting, drawing, or sculpting. The creative process naturally brings people together and creates bonds that extend beyond art sessions. Your program becomes a safe haven where vulnerability transforms into strength through artistic expression.

Getting Started

Learn the Basics: Take courses in art therapy fundamentals, even if just introductory ones. Understanding the difference between art instruction and art therapy is crucial.

Find Your Venue: Partner with senior centers, assisted living facilities, hospitals, or community centers. Many facilities would love this service but lack leadership.

Start Simple: Focus on accessible art forms like watercolor, collage, clay work, or mixed media. The goal is expression, not artistic perfection.

Create Safe Spaces: Establish guidelines that emphasize process over product, respect for all expressions, and confidentiality. Artistic skill isn't required.

Gather Adaptive Supplies: Choose materials that work for various physical abilities – large brushes, adaptive grips, and easy-to-manipulate mediums.

Build Your Toolkit: Develop prompts and exercises that encourage emotional expression. Maybe "favorite memories," "seasons of life," or "gratitude gardens."

Partner with Professionals: Connect with licensed art therapists, social workers, or healthcare providers for guidance and referrals.

The Sweet Rewards

You'll witness incredible transformations, help people process life experiences through creativity, build meaningful connections with participants, and maybe discover your own therapeutic gifts. The emotional healing you will facilitate through art will create ripple effects that extend far beyond your sessions!

BUDGET: $500-$3,000 | TIME: 8-15 HRS/WEEK | DIFFICULTY: INTERMEDIATE

#43 Start a Community Musical Group

Bring People Together Through Music and Community

Starting a community choir or musical group transforms individual voices into powerful collective joy while strengthening relationships between neighbors who might never have connected otherwise, improving everyone's mental well-being through group singing, and showcasing incredible musical talent hiding in your area. This venture brings together people of different ages and backgrounds who discover that making music together builds bonds extending far beyond rehearsal time. You'll be amazed at how quickly strangers become friends when sharing the joyful experience of creating beautiful sounds together.

Getting Started

Gather Your Chorus: Start by finding 8-12 people who love to sing, regardless of experience level. Post on community boards, social media, or ask friends who hum while doing dishes.

Choose Your Style: Will you focus on classic hymns, folk songs, pop hits, or a mix? Consider your group's interests and abilities.

Find Your Space: Scout community centers, churches, libraries, or outdoor pavilions. You need somewhere with decent acoustics and room for everyone.

Start Simple: Begin with familiar songs that most people know. "Amazing Grace," "Country Roads," or classic folk songs work well.

Learn Basic Techniques: Brush up on vocal warm-ups, breathing exercises, and simple harmony arrangements. YouTube tutorials can teach you plenty.

Organize Regular Rehearsals: Weekly meetings work best for building skills and group cohesion. Keep sessions fun and supportive – this isn't American Idol.

Plan Performances: Set goals like performing at local events, retirement homes, or community gatherings. Performance dates motivate practice and give everyone purpose.

The Sweet Rewards

You'll create beautiful music, build lasting friendships, boost everyone's mental and

BUDGET: $200-$1,000 | TIME: 5-10 HRS/WEEK | DIFFICULTY: BEG. TO INTERM.

#44 Learn Glassblowing

Create Stunning Art from Fire, Breath, and 2,000-Degree Glass

Learning glassblowing and creating custom pieces combines demanding technical skill with artistic vision while dramatically sharpening your concentration and producing stunning functional masterpieces. This ancient craft requires working with molten glass at extreme temperatures, demanding complete presence that creates an almost meditative state, resulting in pieces that carry the unmistakable mark of handmade artistry.

Getting Started

Find a Studio: Locate local glassblowing studios that offer classes. Most have all equipment and provide instruction. Many community colleges or art centers offer beginner courses.

Master Safety First: Learn proper protective equipment, studio etiquette, and emergency procedures. Hot glass looks the same as cold glass – this matters!

Start with Basics: Begin with simple forms like paperweights, ornaments, or small bowls. Focus on fundamental techniques like gathering, shaping, and timing.

Understand the Science: Learn about glass composition, temperature control, and annealing (cooling process). Understanding why things work prevents expensive mistakes.

Practice Regularly: Book regular studio time to maintain muscle memory and heat tolerance. Consistency builds confidence with this demanding medium.

Develop Your Style: Experiment with colors, textures, and forms. Maybe you excel at delicate ornaments, bold sculptures, or functional pieces like bowls and vases.

Build Your Collection: Create pieces for gifts, home decoration, or potential sales. Document your progress – improvement happens faster than you think.

Connect with Community: Join local glass artists' groups, attend exhibitions, and learn from experienced makers. The glassblowing community is welcoming and generous with knowledge.

The Sweet Rewards

You'll master an ancient and respected craft, create unique gifts and artwork, develop incredible focus and patience, and become the most interesting person at every party. You'll gain expertise in one of humanity's most ancient and mesmerizing art forms!

BUDGET: $500-$3,000 | TIME: 6-15 HRS/WEEK | DIFFICULTY: INTERM. TO ADV.

#45 Create Functional Blacksmith Art

Channel Your Inner Viking (And Make Things That Last Forever)

Taking up blacksmithing and creating functional art involves mastering the elemental forces of fire and steel while participating in one of humanity's most ancient forms of craftsmanship. This noble craft connects you directly to generations of skilled smiths while building remarkable upper body strength and mental focus that comes from working with materials demanding absolute respect.

Getting Started

Find Your Forge: Look for local blacksmithing clubs, community colleges, or maker spaces with forges. Many areas have active blacksmithing communities eager to teach newcomers.

Learn Safety Protocols: Master proper protective equipment, fire safety, and workshop procedures. Hot metal, sparks, and heavy hammers require serious respect and preparation.

Start with Simple Projects: Begin with basic items like hooks, nails, or simple tools. Focus on fundamental techniques like drawing out, upsetting, and bending before attempting complex pieces.

Understand Your Materials: Learn about different types of steel, proper heating temperatures, and cooling techniques. Understanding metal behavior prevents frustration and waste.

Build Your Strength: Blacksmithing is physically demanding but builds impressive upper body strength and endurance. Start with shorter sessions and gradually increase intensity.

Develop Your Skills: Progress from basic hardware to decorative pieces like plant hangers, gate hardware, kitchen utensils, or artistic sculptures.

Connect with Community: Join local blacksmithing associations, attend demonstrations, and learn from master smiths. The blacksmithing community values tradition and mentorship.

The Sweet Rewards

You'll master an ancient and respected craft, create lasting functional art, develop impressive physical strength, and become the person who can make anything from iron while preserving traditional knowledge for the future!

BUDGET: $500-$3,000 | TIME: 6-15 HRS/WEEK | DIFFICULTY: INTERM. TO ADV.

#46 Learn Fiber Arts

Spin Yarn Into Friendship Gold

Learning fiber arts turns you into a skilled textile artisan while revealing the deeply meditative qualities of rhythmic handwork that calms both mind and spirit, producing beautiful textiles that radiate the unmistakable authenticity only handmade items possess. You'll discover that working with fiber engages both creative and technical abilities, creating useful objects that carry personal character machines cannot replicate.

Getting Started

Choose Your Gateway Craft: Start with one technique that appeals to you. Knitting is portable and immediately useful, weaving creates dramatic fabric, spinning transforms fleece into yarn, dyeing adds magical color, and felting sculpts wool into shapes.

Find Your Fiber Community: Join local guilds, yarn shops, or fiber arts groups. These communities are incredibly welcoming and love sharing knowledge with enthusiastic beginners.

Invest in Quality Tools: Good needles, wheels, or looms make learning easier and more enjoyable. Start basic but choose tools that won't frustrate you as you develop skills.

Learn Traditional Techniques: Take classes, watch online tutorials, or find experienced mentors. Each fiber art has generations of accumulated wisdom worth learning.

Source Quality Materials: Experiment with different fibers – wool, cotton, silk, alpaca, bamboo. Each has unique properties and possibilities.

Start Simple, Dream Big: Begin with basic projects like scarves or dishcloths, then progress to complex patterns, custom garments, or artistic installations.

Document Your Journey: Keep samples, take photos, and track your progress. Improvement in fiber arts is dramatic and worth celebrating.

Share Your Creations: Make gifts, sell at craft fairs, or teach others. Handmade textiles are always appreciated and valued.

The Sweet Rewards

You'll master skills that humans have treasured for millennia, create unique and beautiful textiles and garments, develop incredible focus and patience, and always have meaningful gifts to give!

BUDGET: $200-$2,000 | TIME: 5-20 HRS/WEEK | DIFFICULTY: BEG. TO ADV.

NATURE ADVENTURES

#47 Become a Nature Therapy Guide

Turn Your Love of Nature Walks into Professional Healing Practice

Becoming a nature therapy guide transforms you into a skilled healing facilitator while creating meaningful connections between people and the natural world that often leads to profound personal transformation. This rewarding role allows you to guide stressed individuals through carefully designed outdoor experiences that demonstrate why time in nature provides profound stress relief and emotional restoration that indoor therapy cannot replicate.

Getting Started

Learn the Science: Take certified training in forest bathing, nature therapy, or ecotherapy. Programs like the Association of Nature and Forest Therapy offer comprehensive certification courses.

Understand the Practices: Master techniques like mindful observation, sensory awakening exercises, and guided reflection. These aren't just nature walks – they're structured therapeutic interventions.

Find Your Training Ground: Start practicing in local parks, nature preserves, or urban green spaces. You don't need wilderness – any natural environment can be therapeutic.

Build Your Skills: Learn to read groups, facilitate meaningful discussions, and create safe spaces for emotional processing. Much of nature therapy happens through sharing and reflection.

Develop Your Programs: Create structured sessions for different needs – stress relief, grief processing, mindfulness development, or general wellness. Each session should have clear intentions.

Connect with Healthcare: Partner with therapists, doctors, wellness centers, or hospitals who recognize nature therapy's benefits. Many healthcare providers eagerly refer patients to complementary healing practices.

The Sweet Rewards

You'll combine your love of nature with meaningful service, help people discover profound healing in simple natural experiences, potentially earn income doing what you love, and become part of a growing movement that's revolutionizing how we think about health and wellness.

BUDGET: $1,000-$5,000 | TIME: 10-20 HRS/WEEK | DIFFICULTY: INTERMEDIATE

#48 Get Certified as a Master Gardener

Become Your Local Plant Whisperer and Help Your Neighborhood Thrive

Becoming a Master Gardener combines intensive learning of evidence-based gardening techniques while mastering plant biology, soil chemistry, and ecological relationships, establishing yourself as your community's trusted plant expert who can diagnose problems and recommend solutions. This comprehensive certification transforms casual gardening into serious horticultural knowledge, teaching you not just what to do but why techniques work.

Getting Started

Find Your Program: Contact your local Cooperative Extension office – every state has Master Gardener programs. These university-affiliated programs combine rigorous science with hands-on experience.

Commit to the Training: Expect 60-100 hours of classroom instruction covering soil science, plant pathology, entomology, and sustainable gardening practices. It's like getting a horticultural education without student loans.

Master the Science: Learn about plant biology, soil chemistry, pest management, and disease identification. You'll understand not just what to do, but why practices work.

Complete Your Volunteer Hours: Most programs require 50+ hours of community service in your first year. You might staff plant clinics, teach workshops, or help with community gardens.

Build Your Diagnostic Skills: Learn to identify common plant problems, recommend solutions, and know when to refer people to specialists. You become a plant detective.

Share Your Knowledge: Teach classes, write articles, answer hotline questions, or mentor new gardeners. Your expertise becomes a community resource.

The Sweet Rewards

You'll gain deep scientific understanding of plants and ecosystems, become your community's trusted gardening expert, help others succeed with their gardens, and always have the most gorgeous yard on the block. You'll become the mentor who helps neighbors fall in love with the magic of making things grow!

BUDGET: $200-$800 | TIME: 15-25 HRS/WEEK | DIFFICULTY: INTERMEDIATE

#49 Become a Park Naturalist

Turn Your Nature Walks into Educational Adventures

Training as a park naturalist or interpretive guide transforms you into a skilled nature storyteller while forging meaningful connections between people and the natural world that spark lifelong appreciation for conservation. This role combines scientific knowledge with communication skills, teaching you to translate complex ecological concepts into engaging narratives that make everything from soil formation to bird migration accessible to diverse audiences.

Getting Started

Find Training Programs: Contact your state parks, national parks, nature centers, or environmental organizations. Many offer interpretive guide certification programs combining natural science with communication skills.

Learn Your Local Ecosystem: Study the plants, animals, geology, and history of your area. You'll become an expert on why certain trees grow where they do and which birds migrate seasonally.

Master Interpretive Techniques: Learn to use storytelling, hands-on activities, and guided observation to make nature come alive for visitors. It's part science lesson, part theater.

Practice Your Craft: Start by leading friends and family on nature walks, volunteering at local events, or helping with school groups. Practice makes natural.

Develop Signature Programs: Create specialized tours based on your interests – bird watching, wildflower identification, geological features, or local history connections.

Build Your Communication Skills: Learn to read your audience, adjust your approach for different age groups, and handle questions gracefully.

The Sweet Rewards

You'll share your love of nature with others, help people develop deeper environmental awareness, potentially earn income doing outdoor work you love, and become known as the person who can make any outdoor experience more interesting. You'll inspire people to become better stewards of the natural spaces they've learned to love through your guidance!

BUDGET: $200-$1,500 | TIME: 10-20 HRS/WEEK | DIFFICULTY: BEG. TO INTERM.

#50 Create a Certified Wildlife Habitat

Turn Your Boring Lawn into Wildlife Central

Creating a certified wildlife habitat transforms your yard into a thriving haven for birds, butterflies, and native species while reinforcing local ecological health and contributing to conservation science. Your certified habitat provides essential food, water, shelter, and nesting sites that support biodiversity while reducing maintenance through native plants that thrive naturally.

Getting Started

Research Certification Programs: The National Wildlife Federation offers the most popular certification, but check for local programs too.

Assess Your Current Landscape: Identify existing wildlife-friendly features and areas needing improvement. Even small yards can qualify with strategic planning. Plan Your Food Sources: Include native plants that provide seeds, berries, nectar, and leaves throughout seasons. Add feeders and salt licks for additional nutrition sources.

Create Water Features: Install bird baths, small ponds, or simple dripping water sources. Moving water attracts more species than static containers.

Provide Shelter Options: Plant dense shrubs, create brush piles, install nest boxes, or leave dead tree snags for cavity nesters. Different species need different protection.

Design Nesting Areas: Include host plants for butterfly larvae, nesting boxes for birds, and undisturbed ground areas for small mammals.

Eliminate Pesticides: Switch to organic gardening methods that won't harm visiting wildlife. Healthy ecosystems naturally control pest problems.

Document Your Progress: Take photos, keep species lists, and track seasonal changes. This documentation supports your certification application.

Apply for Certification: Submit required documentation and fees. Display your official sign proudly – you've earned bragging rights!

The Sweet Rewards

You'll support local conservation efforts, enjoy constant wildlife entertainment, reduce yard maintenance, and become the neighborhood's unofficial nature expert while creating a lasting sanctuary that supports wildlife for generations!

BUDGET: $500-$3,000 | TIME: 8-15 HRS/WEEK | DIFFICULTY: INTERMEDIATE

#51 Become a Mushroom Foraging Guide

Transform Forest Walks into Gourmet Treasure Hunts

Learning mycology and becoming a mushroom foraging guide opens up discovering wild edibles while developing ecological skills and potentially identifying valuable gourmet mushrooms. This pursuit teaches you to read forest conditions and safely identify edible species.

Getting Started

Learn from Experts: Take formal mycology courses, join local mushroom clubs, or find experienced mentors. Never eat anything you're not 100% certain about – some mushrooms are seriously dangerous.

Master Identification Skills: Study field guides, learn to use spore prints, and understand key identifying features. Start with easily recognized species before attempting tricky look-alikes.

Know Your Local Species: Research what grows in your area during different seasons. Every region has unique mushroom communities based on climate, soil, and forest types.

Practice Safe Foraging: Learn sustainable harvesting techniques, respect private property, and follow local regulations. Good foragers leave ecosystems healthier than they found them.

Build Your Equipment Kit: Invest in mesh bags, sharp knives, field guides, and magnifying glasses. A wicker basket makes you look professional and allows spores to disperse.

Consider Certification: Some areas offer guide certifications or permits for leading commercial forays. Official credentials build trust with potential clients.

Document Your Finds: Keep detailed records, take photographs, and create maps of productive locations for future reference.

The Sweet Rewards

You'll discover free gourmet food, become an expert in forest ecology, potentially earn income leading tours, and always have the most interesting hobby stories. You'll connect with traditional knowledge that links you to generations of skilled foragers who understood nature's hidden bounty!

BUDGET: $200-$1,000 | TIME: 8-20 HRS/WEEK | DIFFICULTY: INTERMEDIATE

#52 Support Native Local Plants

Turn Your Community into a Haven for Native Species

Becoming a champion for native local plants involves transforming your gardening approach while sparking environmental change in your community and establishing your area as a leader in sustainable landscaping. This role allows you to demonstrate how native plants support wildlife, reduce water usage, and create beautiful landscapes while becoming an educator helping your community restore local habitats.

Getting Started

Learn Your Local Flora: Study which plants are truly native to your specific region. Take courses through native plant societies, botanical gardens, or cooperative extension programs.

Transform Your Own Landscape: Replace lawn and exotic plants with native alternatives. Document the process, track wildlife increases, and photograph seasonal changes to show others the benefits.

Start Teaching Others: Host garden tours, give presentations to neighborhood groups, HOA meetings, or write articles for local publications. Share both the environmental benefits and beauty of native landscapes, addressing common concerns about "messy" native plants.

Partner with Organizations: Connect with native plant societies, environmental groups, conservation organizations, and progressive HOA boards. Collaborate on community projects, educational events, and policy updates that support native landscaping.

Advocate for Policy Changes: Work with local governments to promote native plant requirements in public landscaping and offer homeowner incentives while restricting invasive species sales. Engage HOA boards to update restrictive covenants that currently prevent native landscaping.

Mentor New Gardeners: Help neighbors transition to native plants, provide ongoing support, and celebrate their successes.

The Sweet Rewards

You'll regenerate local natural systems, create habitat that supports diverse wildlife populations, reduce irrigation and care costs for all neighbors, and become the person credited with making your community an example of ecological excellence!

BUDGET: $300-$2,000 | TIME: 8-20 HRS/WEEK | DIFFICULTY: INTERMEDIATE

#53 Create a Network of Hiking Trails

Become Your Area's Trail Blazer (Literally and Figuratively)

Building and maintaining hiking trails involves hands-on construction while establishing access points that connect people with nature and positioning yourself as someone who shapes how residents experience outdoor spaces. You become a steward ensuring trails remain safe and accessible to families, seniors, and people with varying fitness levels.

Getting Started

Scout Your Territory: Identify potential trail corridors through parks, greenbelts, abandoned rail lines, or connecting existing paths. Look for routes that link neighborhoods, schools, or commercial areas.

Get Official Support: Contact parks departments, land trusts, or property owners about trail development.

Learn Trail Building Basics: Take courses through hiking clubs, land management agencies, or trail organizations. Proper trail design prevents erosion, protects wildlife, and ensures longevity.

Recruit Your Trail Crew: Find volunteers who enjoy outdoor work and community building.

Plan Your Route Network: Design trails for different skill levels and purposes – maybe easy walks for families, challenging hikes for athletes, or loops that return to parking areas.

Acquire Proper Tools: Invest in basic trail building equipment like hand tools, marking supplies, and safety gear. Many land management agencies loan tools to volunteer groups.

Create Maintenance Systems: Establish regular inspection schedules, seasonal cleanup events, and reporting procedures for problems. Ongoing maintenance keeps trails safe and enjoyable.

Build Usage and Support: Create simple maps, promote your trails through local groups, and organize guided hikes to build community awareness and appreciation.

The Sweet Rewards

You'll develop trail systems that benefit future generations, promote community health through outdoor opportunities, organize an enthusiastic volunteer base, and become known as the champion who made nature truly available to everyone!

BUDGET: $500-$5,000 | TIME: 10-25 HRS/WEEK | DIFFICULTY: INTERMEDIATE

#54 Create a Backyard Bird Sanctuary

Create a Wildlife Haven That Supports Global Conservation Research

Creating a backyard bird sanctuary combines attracting beautiful visitors while supporting declining bird populations and participating in conservation through citizen science. You'll discover your sanctuary becomes a living laboratory where you observe behavior and contribute to research.

Getting Started

Design Your Bird Paradise: Plan layers of vegetation from ground covers to canopy trees. Different species prefer different heights, so variety attracts diversity. Include native plants that provide seeds, berries, and insects throughout seasons.

Install Water Features: Birds need fresh water for drinking and bathing. Consider dripping fountains, shallow basins, or small ponds, as moving water attracts more species than static containers.

Provide Diverse Food Sources: Offer multiple feeder types with different seeds, suet, and nectar. Native plants provide natural food, while feeders supplement during harsh weather or breeding seasons.

Create Nesting Opportunities: Install various nest boxes for different species, plant dense shrubs for natural nesting, and provide nesting materials like twigs, moss, and pet fur.

Join Citizen Science Projects: Participate in eBird, Christmas Bird Count, or Project FeederWatch. Your observations contribute to global databases that guide conservation decisions.

Learn Identification Skills: Study field guides, use bird identification apps, and join local birding groups. The more you can identify, the more valuable your data becomes.

Document Your Visitors: Keep detailed records of species, numbers, behaviors, and seasonal patterns. Take photos and notes about unusual sightings or behaviors.

Share Your Success: Host bird walks, write about your sanctuary, or mentor other bird enthusiasts. Your passion inspires others to create bird-friendly spaces.

The Sweet Rewards

You'll support conservation, contribute to research, and become your neighborhood's bird expert while demonstrating how individual actions make real conservation differences!

BUDGET: $300-$2,000 | TIME: 5-15 HRS/WEEK | DIFFICULTY: BEG. TO INTERM.

#55 Teach Wilderness Survival Skills

Become the Wilderness Expert Who Makes Every Adventure Better

Learning wilderness survival skills builds emergency preparedness while connecting you to ancestral knowledge and developing confidence in natural environments. This education teaches you to find water, create fire without matches, build shelters, and identify edible plants. You'll master skills that work regardless of technology failures while gaining confidence from handling outdoor situations using only your knowledge and nature's resources.

Getting Started

Master Fire Creation: Learn fire-starting techniques like bow drills, flint and steel, and fire plows that don't rely on matches or lighters. Fire creation is crucial since it provides warmth, enables cooking, purifies water, and offers psychological comfort.

Study Shelter Building: Learn to construct weatherproof shelters using natural materials. Practice debris huts, lean-tos, and emergency shelters for different climates and seasons.

Learn Water Procurement: Master finding, collecting, and purifying water from natural sources. Understand solar stills, tree taps, dew collection, and various filtration methods.

Develop Foraging Skills: Study edible plants, mushrooms, and insects in your region. Learn sustainable harvesting techniques and proper identification to avoid dangerous mistakes.

Practice Navigation: Master compass and map reading, plus natural navigation using sun, stars, and landscape features. GPS batteries die, but celestial navigation works forever.

Build Tool-Making Skills: Learn to create useful tools from natural materials – knives from stone, cordage from plants, and containers from bark or gourds.

Take Formal Training: Enroll in wilderness survival courses, primitive skills workshops, or bushcraft programs. Hands-on instruction prevents dangerous errors.

The Sweet Rewards

You'll gain confidence in outdoor situations, connect with natural environments, develop problem-solving skills, and become the person others trust for outdoor wisdom. You'll master skills that work regardless of technology failures or equipment breakdowns!

BUDGET: $300-$2,000 | TIME: 8-20 HRS/WEEK | DIFFICULTY: INTERM. TO ADV.

#56 Start a Beekeeping Program

Become the Neighborhood's Honey Hero

Starting a community beekeeping program transforms solitary beekeeping into collective action while developing shared expertise and combining resources to make beekeeping more accessible. This approach allows beginners to learn from experienced members while sharing equipment costs, creating a supportive community where members help each other and educate the public about pollinator importance.

Getting Started

Learn from Experts: Take formal beekeeping courses through agricultural extensions, local associations, or experienced mentors. Understanding bee behavior prevents stings and ensures colony health.

Find Your Bee Space: Scout locations for hives – community gardens, schools, parks, or members' properties. Bees need morning sun, wind protection, and nearby water sources.

Start Small but Smart: Begin with 2-3 hives to learn management techniques. Healthy colonies can produce 30-60 pounds of honey annually while supporting local plant life.

Gather Essential Equipment: Invest in hives, protective gear, smokers, and extraction equipment. Many programs share expensive items like honey extractors among members.

Build Your Bee Team: Recruit neighbors interested in pollinators, gardening, or sustainable living. Some members keep hives while others help with maintenance, marketing, or education.

Create Learning Opportunities: Host workshops on bee biology, hive management, and honey extraction. Many people love learning about these fascinating creatures.

Share the Bounty: Distribute honey among participants, sell at farmers markets, or donate to local food banks. Fresh, local honey creates instant community ambassadors.

The Sweet Rewards

You'll participate in pollinator conservation, harvest liquid gold from your own hives, foster connections with environmental stewards, and gain appreciation for the intricate relationships between bees, plants, and human food systems!

BUDGET: $800-$3,000 | TIME: 8-15 HRS/WEEK | DIFFICULTY: INTERMEDIATE

#57 Create a Butterfly Garden

Transform Your Yard into Butterfly Paradise

Creating a butterfly garden and breeding program transforms your property into a butterfly sanctuary while exploring metamorphosis and supporting vulnerable species facing population declines. This project teaches you to provide host plants and nectar sources while establishing protected areas where caterpillars develop safely. You become both gardener and conservationist, creating conditions for successful reproduction.

Getting Started

Research Your Local Species: Study which butterflies are native to your area and what plants they need. Different species require specific host plants for egg-laying and caterpillar development.

Design for Complete Life Cycles: Plant nectar sources for adult butterflies and host plants for caterpillars. Monarchs need milkweed, swallowtails prefer parsley family plants, and painted ladies love thistles.

Create Seasonal Succession: Plan blooms from early spring through late fall. Butterflies need consistent nectar sources throughout their active season.

Provide Essential Features: Include shallow water sources, sunny open areas for basking, and wind protection.

Eliminate Pesticides: Switch to organic gardening methods that won't harm butterflies or their larvae. Healthy gardens naturally balance pest problems.

Document Your Success: Keep records of species, numbers, and breeding success. Contribute data to citizen science projects tracking butterfly populations.

Share Your Knowledge: Host garden tours, teach children about butterfly life cycles, or mentor other gardeners. Your success inspires others to create butterfly habitats.

Connect with Conservation: Partner with local butterfly organizations, participate in tagging programs, or support habitat restoration projects.

The Sweet Rewards

You'll support threatened species, enjoy constant natural entertainment, and become known as the neighborhood's butterfly expert while creating educational opportunities for children.

BUDGET: $300-$2,000 | TIME: 6-15 HRS/WEEK | DIFFICULTY: INTERMEDIATE

#58 Become a Certified Arborist

Transform from Tree Hugger to Tree Doctor (And Save Urban Forests)

Becoming a certified arborist involves mastering tree biology and disease management while understanding urban forestry challenges and providing expert care that keeps communities green for future generations. This certification teaches you to assess tree health, identify problems, and make informed decisions about pruning or removal that balance safety with environmental benefits.

Getting Started

Study Tree Science: Learn tree biology, disease identification, soil science, and pruning techniques through formal arboriculture programs. Many community colleges offer comprehensive courses.

Gain Field Experience: Work with established tree care companies, volunteer with urban forestry programs, or assist certified arborists to build practical skills and understanding.

Pursue Certification: Take the International Society of Arboriculture certification exam covering tree biology, diagnosis, treatment, and safety. Continuing education maintains credentials.

Master Safety Protocols: Learn proper climbing techniques, equipment use, and hazard assessment. Tree work can be dangerous – safety knowledge protects you and others.

Develop Diagnostic Skills: Practice identifying common tree problems, pest issues, and environmental stresses. Learn when trees can be saved versus when removal is necessary.

Stay Current: Attend workshops, join professional organizations, and keep up with new research in tree care techniques and urban forestry practices.

Educate Others: Teach proper tree care, lead community tree walks, or help develop municipal tree ordinances. Share knowledge that helps communities value their urban forests.

The Sweet Rewards

You'll preserve green spaces, provide environmental services, earn potential income, and save beloved trees from unnecessary removal.

BUDGET: $1,000-$5,000 | TIME: 15-30 HRS/WEEK | DIFFICULTY: ADVANCED

#59 Start a Nature Photography Business

Create Art That Protects the Natural World

Starting a nature photography business for conservation involves using visual storytelling to protect ecosystems and raise environmental awareness while building a photographic legacy that contributes to preserving nature. This business combines artistic passion with advocacy, allowing you to document endangered species and habitats while generating income from sales and workshops.

Getting Started

Master Your Equipment: Learn advanced camera techniques, lighting principles, and composition rules. Whether using professional gear or high-end smartphones, technical skill makes conservation images more impactful.

Study Animal Behavior: Understand your subjects' habits, feeding times, and seasonal patterns. Great wildlife photography requires patience and knowledge, not just expensive lenses.

Learn Ethical Practices: Follow guidelines that prioritize animal welfare over getting the shot. Never disturb nests, use flash inappropriately, or stress wildlife for photographs.

Find Your Conservation Focus: Choose specific causes – maybe documenting local endangered species, showcasing habitat restoration, or capturing climate change impacts on ecosystems.

Develop Multiple Revenue Streams: Sell prints at nature centers, license images to publications, offer guided photo tours, or create educational materials featuring your work.

Share Your Mission: Use social media, local exhibitions, and community presentations to combine beautiful imagery with conservation education.

Document Local Issues: Focus on environmental challenges in your area – pollution impacts, habitat loss, or species recovery success stories.

The Sweet Rewards

You'll combine artistic passion with meaningful conservation work, potentially earn income doing what you love, build awareness for important causes, and create a visual legacy that helps protect the natural world!

BUDGET: $1,000-$8,000 | TIME: 15-30 HRS/WEEK | DIFFICULTY: INTERM. TO ADV.

#60 Learn to Identify Local Flora and Fauna

Master the Art of Reading Nature

Learning to identify and catalog local flora and fauna involves understanding ecosystems while tracking environmental changes and building a database that helps scientists monitor biological health. You become a citizen scientist whose observations contribute to biodiversity assessments guiding conservation decisions.

Getting Started

Master Field Guides: Start with regional plant and animal identification guides. Learn to use identification keys, understand scientific nomenclature, and recognize key distinguishing features for different species groups.

Choose Your Focus Areas: Begin with one or two groups like birds and wildflowers, then expand to include mammals, insects, trees, or fungi. Specializing initially builds confidence and expertise.

Use Modern Tools: Download apps like iNaturalist, eBird, or Seek that help with identification and automatically contribute your sightings to scientific databases.

Join Local Groups: Connect with naturalist clubs, Audubon chapters, or native plant societies where experienced members share knowledge and verify difficult identifications.

Create Systematic Records: Develop databases tracking species locations, abundance, seasonal timing, and habitat preferences. Consistent methodology makes your data scientifically valuable.

Explore Different Habitats: Survey forests, wetlands, grasslands, and urban areas to document the full range of local biodiversity. Each habitat supports unique species communities.

Share Your Discoveries: Submit records to citizen science projects, contribute to local nature guides, or lead identification workshops for other community members.

Monitor Changes Over Time: Track species presence, abundance, and seasonal timing year after year to document environmental changes and species responses.

The Sweet Rewards

You'll become an expert on local biodiversity, contribute valuable scientific data, never lack for outdoor entertainment, and become the neighborhood's go-to nature expert.

BUDGET: $200-$1,500 | TIME: 8-20 HRS/WEEK | DIFFICULTY: BEG. TO INTERM.

#61 Teach Outdoor Skills to Urban Youth

Help City Kids Discover They're Born Adventurers

Starting a program teaching outdoor skills to urban youth transforms recreation into powerful education while developing essential life skills and establishing connections between young people and natural environments. This program introduces urban kids to wilderness skills while teaching problem-solving and resilience. You become a bridge helping young people discover capabilities.

Getting Started

Partner with Youth Organizations: Connect with schools, community centers, youth groups, or after-school programs serving urban kids. Many organizations want outdoor programming but lack qualified instructors.

Design Age-Appropriate Curriculum: Plan activities for different skill levels – maybe basic camping for beginners, advanced wilderness skills for experienced participants, or specialized programs like urban foraging or nature photography.

Start with Basics: Teach fundamental skills like fire building, shelter construction, water purification, and basic first aid. Build complexity gradually as participants gain confidence and competence.

Emphasize Safety: Develop comprehensive safety protocols, proper supervision ratios, and emergency procedures. Urban kids may need extra attention to outdoor hazards they haven't encountered.

Make It Relevant: Connect outdoor skills to urban life – maybe urban gardening, rooftop beekeeping, or finding nature in city environments. Help kids see how wilderness skills apply to their daily world.

Build Mentorship: Create ongoing relationships rather than one-time workshops. Regular programming allows deep skill development and lasting impact.

Celebrate Achievements: Create recognition systems, skill badges, or demonstrations where participants can show families what they've learned.

The Sweet Rewards

You'll open new worlds for young people, build their confidence, and become the adult who made the outdoors accessible while creating lasting memories and developing skills that serve them throughout their lives!

BUDGET: $500-$3,000 | TIME: 8-20 HRS/WEEK | DIFFICULTY: INTERMEDIATE

#62 Learn Herbalism

Turn Your Backyard into Nature's Pharmacy

Creating a medicinal herb garden and learning herbalism establishes your natural apothecary while exploring traditional healing practices and gaining self-sufficiency in addressing minor ailments naturally. This practice teaches you to grow, harvest, and prepare therapeutic herbs while developing expertise in plant identification and safe preparation methods.

Getting Started

Study Before You Plant: Learn about medicinal herbs through reputable courses, books, or experienced herbalists. Understanding proper identification, preparation, and dosages is crucial for safety.

Choose Your Healing Plants: Start with gentle, well-researched herbs like echinacea for immune support, lavender for relaxation, calendula for skin healing, and chamomile for digestion.

Master Growing Techniques: Learn organic cultivation methods, proper harvesting timing, and post-harvest handling. Medicinal potency depends on growing and processing quality.

Learn Preparation Methods: Study how to make teas, tinctures, salves, and other herbal preparations. Different methods extract different plant compounds.

Connect with Community: Join herbalism groups, attend workshops, or find experienced mentors. The herbalist community values traditional knowledge and safe practices.

Practice Ethical Wildcrafting: If foraging wild herbs, learn sustainable harvesting techniques and proper plant identification. Never harvest endangered species.

Respect Limitations: Understand when professional medical care is needed. Herbalism complements but doesn't replace proper medical treatment for serious conditions.

The Sweet Rewards

You'll develop self-reliance for minor health issues, connect with ancient healing wisdom, create a beautiful and functional garden, and become the neighborhood expert on natural remedies!

BUDGET: $300-$2,000 | TIME: 8-15 HRS/WEEK | DIFFICULTY: INTERMEDIATE

#63 Start an Outdoor Education Program

Prove That Adventure Has No Expiration Date

Starting an outdoor education program for seniors transforms outdoor time into meaningful experiences while designing age-appropriate adventures and proving that outdoor skills can thrive regardless of age. You become an advocate for active aging, demonstrating that older learners are often the most engaged participants.

Getting Started

Partner with Senior Organizations: Connect with senior centers, retirement communities, adult education programs, or hiking clubs that serve older adults. Many organizations want outdoor programming but need experienced leadership.

Design Age-Appropriate Activities: Plan programs considering physical abilities, interests, and experience levels. Maybe gentle hiking, nature photography, bird watching, gardening workshops, or outdoor survival skills adapted for seniors.

Address Safety Concerns: Develop protocols for medical conditions, mobility issues, and emergency procedures. Create programs that feel challenging but safe for participants with varying fitness levels.

Start with Popular Topics: Offer programs on local nature identification, seasonal outdoor activities, or combining outdoor time with health benefits. Build from interests people already express.

Adapt to Seasons: Plan year-round programming that works with weather and seasonal interests. Indoor sessions during harsh weather, outdoor adventures during pleasant conditions.

Build Confidence Gradually: Start with easy, accessible locations and activities. Build skills and comfort levels before attempting more challenging adventures.

Include Expert Guests: Invite naturalists, park rangers, or outdoor professionals to share specialized knowledge. Variety keeps programs interesting and educational.

Celebrate Achievements: Recognize participants' progress, new skills learned, or personal milestones reached. Positive reinforcement encourages continued participation.

The Sweet Rewards

You'll build networks of adventurous seniors, help participants overcome limiting beliefs about aging, and earn recognition as someone who redefines what's possible in later life!

BUDGET: $300-$2,000 | TIME: 8-15 HRS/WEEK | DIFFICULTY: INTERMEDIATE

TRAVEL ADVENTURES

#64 Take a Cross-Country RV Trip

Turn Your Golden Years into the Great American Adventure

Taking a cross-country RV trip to visit all national parks transforms travel into an epic American adventure while experiencing spectacular landscapes at your own pace and creating lasting memories. You become part of a special RV community enjoying the freedom of carrying your home wherever adventure calls.

Getting Started

Choose Your RV: Rent first to test different sizes and styles. Factor in your driving comfort and campground accessibility.

Plan Your Route: Map efficient circuits connecting multiple parks. Consider seasonal weather, elevation changes, and reservation requirements. Some parks require bookings months in advance.

Master RV Basics: Learn about hookups, waste management, propane systems, and basic maintenance. Take an RV driving course – these vehicles handle differently than cars.

Get Your Parks Pass: Purchase the America the Beautiful Annual Pass for significant savings. At age 62, upgrade to the lifetime Senior Pass for even better value.

Prepare for Camping: Stock essential supplies, plan meal strategies, and understand campground etiquette. Many parks offer full hookups, while others provide primitive camping experiences.

Plan Extended Stays: Don't rush – spend multiple days at larger parks to fully experience hiking trails, ranger programs, and wildlife viewing opportunities.

Document Your Journey: Keep detailed travel logs, collect park stamps in a passport book, and create photo albums. Your adventures become treasured memories and great stories.

Connect with Community: Join RV clubs, attend campground social hours, and participate in ranger programs. The RV community is welcoming and full of travel wisdom.

The Sweet Rewards

You'll immerse yourself in America's most awe-inspiring natural environments, become a seasoned road warrior, encounter fellow adventurers who become lifelong friends, and build a collection of experiences that make you feel truly accomplished!

BUDGET: $15,000-$75,000 | TIME: 3-12 MONTHS | DIFFICULTY: INTERMEDIATE

#65 Go on a Photography Safari in Africa

Capture the Wild Kingdom Through Your Lens

Going on a photography safari in Africa means immersing yourself in one of Earth's last great wildlife spectacles and mastering challenging photography conditions while potentially becoming the person whose stunning photos make others jealous.

Getting Started

Choose Your Destination: Research different regions – Kenya's Masai Mara for the migration, Tanzania's Serengeti for classic safari scenes, Botswana's Okavango Delta for water-based wildlife, or South Africa's Kruger for variety and accessibility.

Select Photography-Focused Tours: Book specialized photo safaris with expert guides who understand animal behavior and lighting conditions. These tours prioritize photography opportunities over general sightseeing.

Master Your Equipment: Practice with telephoto lenses, understand camera settings for action shots, and learn to work in challenging light conditions. African wildlife won't wait for you to figure out your camera.

Study Animal Behavior: Learn about feeding times, migration patterns, and seasonal behaviors. Great wildlife photography requires understanding your subjects, not just technical skills.

Consider Seasonal Timing: Research when to visit for specific experiences – calving season, river crossings, or optimal weather conditions for your chosen destination.

Budget Realistically: Quality photography safaris are significant investments. Factor in flights, accommodations, park fees, equipment, and post-trip photo processing.

Prepare Physically: Safari days can be long and physically demanding. Build stamina for early mornings, long vehicle rides, and carrying camera equipment.

Study the Culture: Learn about local customs, conservation efforts, and responsible tourism practices. Respectful visitors create better experiences for everyone.

The Sweet Rewards

You'll capture once-in-a-lifetime images, experience Africa's incredible wildlife firsthand, improve your photography skills dramatically, and return with captivating stories while supporting conservation through responsible tourism!

BUDGET: $8,000-$25,000+ | TIME: 2-4 WEEKS | DIFFICULTY: INTERMEDIATE

#66 Take a Cooking Tour Through Italy

Turn Your Kitchen Skills into Passport Adventures

Taking a cooking tour through Italy or France means immersing yourself in centuries-old culinary traditions, learning authentic techniques from master chefs, and creating memories that inspire your home cooking. This journey takes you into family kitchens where you'll discover how real pasta is made and what makes regional ingredients special.

Getting Started

Choose Your Culinary Destination: Research regions known for specific cuisines – Tuscany for rustic Italian fare, Provence for French country cooking, or Sicily for unique Mediterranean fusion. Each area offers distinct flavors and techniques.

Select Hands-On Programs: Book tours that emphasize cooking instruction over restaurant dining. Look for small groups, multiple cooking sessions, and market visits where you select ingredients.

Research Your Teachers: Seek programs led by local chefs, cookbook authors, or culinary families. The best experiences come from passionate instructors who share cultural context with recipes.

Document Everything: Bring recipe notebooks, take photos of techniques, and ask questions about substitutions for ingredients unavailable at home.

Connect with Fellow Foodies: Cooking tours attract passionate food lovers. Build friendships that continue beyond the trip through recipe sharing and dinner exchanges.

Extend Your Learning: Look for tours that provide recipe collections, online follow-up sessions, or connections to ingredient suppliers.

Plan Your Return: Consider how you'll use new skills – hosting dinner parties, teaching friends, or even starting your own cooking classes.

Embrace the Culture: Participate in local traditions, visit family kitchens, and understand how food connects to regional history and customs.

The Sweet Rewards

You'll master authentic techniques from legendary culinary regions, gain confidence with complex recipes, create unforgettable travel memories, and become the cook whose dinner invitations are treasured!

BUDGET: $3,000-$15,000 | TIME: 1-3 WEEKS | DIFFICULTY: BEG. TO INTERM.

#67 Become a Touring Sports or Music Fan

Turn Your Fandom into the Adventure of a Lifetime

Following your favorites on the road transforms travel into the ultimate fan adventure while immersing yourself in fandom culture and creating incredible memories that forge deeper connections to music or sports than you ever imagined possible!

Getting Started

Choose Your Adventure: Pick an artist on a major tour or a sports team with an exciting season schedule. Consider factors like venue types, travel distances, and whether you prefer intimate concerts or massive stadium experiences.

Plan Your Route: Map out tour dates or game schedules, book accommodations in advance, and plan efficient travel routes between cities.

Connect with Fan Communities: Join online forums, social media groups, or fan clubs. Other devoted fans share insider tips, coordinate meetups, and enhance the entire experience.

Budget for the Experience: Factor in tickets, travel, accommodations, meals, and merchandise. Consider splurging on VIP packages or premium seats – you're living the dream!

Pack Smart: Bring comfortable shoes, weather-appropriate clothing, and essentials for different venues. Consider portable phone chargers, small bags that meet venue requirements, and comfortable travel gear.

Embrace the Culture: Learn about each city you visit, try local food, and explore attractions between shows or games. Make it a cultural adventure, not just entertainment.

Meet Fellow Fans: Strike up conversations in lines, share experiences, and maybe make lifelong friendships with people who share your passion.

The Sweet Rewards

You'll experience your passion with intensity casual fans never achieve, create memories spanning different cities and once-in-a-generation performances, and return with incredible tales of cross-country adventures and perfect nights when being a true fan paid off unexpectedly!

BUDGET: $5,000-$25,000+ | TIME: 2-8 WEEKS | DIFFICULTY: BEGINNER

#68 Go on a Learning Vacation

Make Every Journey a Masterclass in Something Fascinating

Going on a learning vacation means selecting travel experiences designed to teach you new subjects while exploring destinations that serve as your classroom. These educational adventures allow you to learn from world-class experts in memorable settings.

Getting Started

Explore Road Scholar Programs: This nonprofit organization offers educational travel programs specifically for adults 50+. Choose from archaeology expeditions, cultural immersions, natural history tours, or behind-the-scenes experiences at world-class institutions.

Choose Your Passion Subject: Pick topics that genuinely excite you – maybe art history in Renaissance Italy, marine biology in the Caribbean, Civil War battlefields, astronomy in dark-sky locations, or photography workshops in stunning landscapes.

Consider Different Formats: Look for hands-on workshops, expert-led tours, university-sponsored programs, or specialty travel companies focusing on education. Some combine lectures with field experiences.

Research Your Instructors: Seek programs led by recognized experts, university professors, or passionate specialists. The best learning vacations combine deep knowledge with engaging teaching styles.

Plan for Small Groups: Look for programs with limited participants that encourage interaction, questions, and personalized attention. Avoid large tour bus experiences that rush through topics.

Prepare Your Mind: Do some preliminary reading about your chosen subject and destination. Background knowledge makes the experience richer and helps you ask better questions.

Pack Learning Tools: Bring notebooks, good pens, portable cameras, and maybe recording apps for capturing insights. Document your discoveries for later reflection.

The Sweet Rewards

You'll satisfy your curiosity about fascinating subjects, gain expert knowledge you can't get from books alone, meet like-minded lifelong learners, and return home with stories that make everyone jealous of your adventures!

BUDGET: $2,000-$8,000+ | TIME: 1-3 WEEKS | DIFFICULTY: BEG. TO INTERM.

#69 Take a Train Journey

Master the Art of Slow Travel and Scenic Routes

Taking a train journey across multiple countries transforms travel into a relaxing adventure while savoring movement at a leisurely pace, enjoying countryside views hidden from highway travelers, and developing meaningful connections that hurried air travel never permits.

Getting Started

Choose Your Epic Route: Research legendary train journeys – the Trans-Siberian Railway across Russia, Eurail passes through Europe, the Canadian across Canada, The Empire Builder from Chicago to Seattle, or the Indian Pacific across Australia. Each offers unique landscapes and cultural experiences.

Plan Your Passes and Tickets: Purchase rail passes that allow flexibility, or book specific routes well in advance for popular journeys. Consider first-class compartments for longer trips – you're worth the comfort.

Prepare for Extended Travel: Pack strategically with comfortable clothes, entertainment, and essentials for days onboard. Bring books, journals, cameras, and whatever helps you relax and enjoy the journey.

Research Your Route: Study the countries, cities, and landscapes you'll traverse. Understanding what you're seeing enhances the experience and helps you plan stops.

Plan Strategic Stops: Don't rush – spend days or weeks in interesting cities along your route. Train travel works best when you have time to explore destinations, not just pass through them.

Embrace Train Culture: Learn dining car etiquette, understand compartment protocols, and be open to conversations with fellow travelers. Train journeys create unique social experiences.

Consider Seasonal Timing: Research optimal seasons for your chosen route – stunning autumn foliage, comfortable weather, or avoiding extreme conditions.

The Sweet Rewards

You'll see multiple countries from unique perspectives, meet international travelers, experience the romance of classic rail travel, and create joyful memories of amazing places some people only dream of seeing!

BUDGET: $3,000-$15,000+ | TIME: 2-8 WEEKS | DIFFICULTY: BEGINNER

#70 Go Glamping in Unique Locations

Sleep Under the Stars with Five-Star Comfort

Glamping combines "glamorous" and "camping" to create accommodations that let you experience nature without sacrificing comfort. Think safari tents with real beds, treehouses with electricity, or yurts with gourmet kitchens.

Getting Started

Choose Your Unique Accommodation: Research extraordinary options – treehouses in Costa Rica, luxury safari tents in Montana, yurts in Utah, converted train cars in Colorado, or floating cabins in Canada. Each offers different adventures and comfort levels.

Consider Your Interests: Match accommodations to activities you love – wine country glamping for foodies, desert yurts for stargazers, forest treehouses for wildlife watchers, or lakeside cabins for anglers.

Research Seasonal Timing: Plan visits during optimal weather and activity seasons. Some locations offer year-round appeal, while others shine during specific months.

Book Well in Advance: Popular glamping sites fill quickly, especially during peak seasons. Unique accommodations often have limited availability and loyal repeat customers.

Pack Appropriately: Bring clothes for outdoor activities plus comfortable indoor wear. Most glamping includes linens and basic amenities, but check what's provided versus what you need.

Embrace the Setting: Participate in activities you can't do at home – maybe stargazing in dark-sky locations, wildlife photography, or simply enjoying silence away from city noise.

Connect with Nature: Use this comfortable outdoor time to really observe natural settings, wildlife, and seasonal changes often missed in traditional travel.

Consider Different Regions: Try glamping in various climates and landscapes – deserts, mountains, forests, or coastal areas each offer unique experiences and accommodation styles.

The Sweet Rewards

You'll experience stunning natural locations in comfort, try unique accommodations, enjoy outdoor adventures without camping hassles, and create magical memories in extraordinary places!

BUDGET: $200-$800 PER NIGHT | TIME: 2-7 DAYS/TRIP | DIFFICULTY: BEGINNER

#71 Join a Volunteer Vacation

Turn Your Travel into Life-Changing Impact

Joining a volunteer vacation combines meaningful service with travel adventure, allowing you to contribute expertise while experiencing destinations authentically and creating lasting impact in communities that need assistance. You'll discover that volunteer travel creates deeper satisfaction than sightseeing alone, using your skills to help others while building relationships that continue after you return home.

Getting Started

Choose Your Passion Project: Research diverse opportunities – wildlife conservation in Costa Rica, teaching English in rural schools, marine turtle research, archaeological digs, disaster relief rebuilding, medical missions, or environmental restoration projects.

Select Reputable Organizations: Partner with established groups like Global Volunteers, Earthwatch Institute, Cross-Cultural Solutions, or habitat-focused nonprofits. Avoid programs that exploit local communities or provide minimal benefit.

Match Skills to Needs: Use your professional background – maybe financial literacy training, healthcare support, construction expertise, educational instruction, or technology skills for underserved communities.

Research Cultural Context: Learn about destinations, local customs, and community needs before traveling. Understanding context makes your contribution more effective and culturally sensitive.

Prepare for Real Work: Expect physical demands, basic accommodations, and challenging conditions. Volunteer vacations are working trips, not luxury travel with a service component.

Plan Extended Stays: Meaningful impact requires time. Consider 2-4 week commitments that allow relationship building and project completion rather than brief symbolic visits.

Budget Realistically: Quality volunteer programs require significant investment. Factor in program fees, travel costs, and personal expenses while ensuring your money supports legitimate impact.

The Sweet Rewards

You'll make tangible differences in communities worldwide, gain deep cultural understanding, use your skills meaningfully, and return with perspectives that transform how you see both travel and service!

BUDGET: $2,000-$8,000+ | TIME: 1-6 WEEKS | DIFFICULTY: INTERM. TO ADV.

#72 Go on a Guided Hiking Trip

Transform Your Limits on the World's Most Epic Trails

Going on a guided hiking trip to legendary destinations transforms ordinary exercise into an extraordinary journey through iconic landscapes while experiencing ancient paths that connect you to centuries of history and creating unforgettable achievements that make every local trail seem like a warm-up.

Getting Started

Choose Your Epic Journey: Research iconic hiking destinations – the Camino de Santiago across Spain for spiritual reflection, Machu Picchu in Peru for ancient wonder, the Tour du Mont Blanc for alpine beauty, or the Milford Track in New Zealand for pristine wilderness.

Select Quality Guides: Book with established companies that provide experienced guides, proper support, and safety protocols. Look for small groups, good reviews, and clear fitness requirements.

Assess Your Fitness: Start training months in advance with regular walking, hiking, and cardio exercise. Most guided trips accommodate moderate fitness levels but require preparation.

Plan Your Timing: Research optimal seasons for your chosen destination. Weather, crowds, and trail conditions vary dramatically throughout the year.

Prepare Your Gear: Invest in quality hiking boots, comfortable clothing, and essential equipment. Many companies provide detailed packing lists and gear recommendations.

Understand the Experience: Learn about daily distances, elevation changes, accommodation types, and cultural highlights. Set realistic expectations for physical demands and comfort levels.

Embrace the Journey: Guided hikes often emphasize personal growth, cultural immersion, and spiritual reflection beyond just reaching destinations.

Prepare Mentally: These hikes often challenge more than physical fitness. Prepare for weather, discomfort, and the mental resilience needed for multi-day adventures.

The Sweet Rewards

You'll accomplish bucket-list adventures, experience profound personal growth, and become the person whose hiking stories inspire others to push their own boundaries!

BUDGET: $2,000-$8,000+ | TIME: 1-3 WEEKS | DIFFICULTY: INTERM. TO ADV.

#73 Experience the Northern Lights

Witness Nature's Most Magical Celestial Show

Experiencing the Northern Lights in Iceland, Alaska, or Scandinavia provides a front-row seat to one of nature's most incredible light shows while connecting you to ancient natural rhythms that have amazed humans for thousands of years. You'll stand in pristine wilderness watching the aurora paint the heavens with colors no photograph can capture.

Getting Started

Choose Your Aurora Destination: Research Iceland for accessible viewing with comfortable accommodations, Alaska for wilderness experiences with incredible night skies or Scandinavian destinations for a northern European cultural experience. Each offers unique advantages and cultural experiences.

Plan for Prime Season: Visit between October and March when nights are longest and darkest. Peak activity often occurs around equinoxes, but solar activity varies unpredictably.

Book Aurora-Focused Tours: Select operators specializing in Northern Lights experiences who understand weather patterns, optimal locations, and backup plans for cloudy nights.

Prepare for Waiting: Aurora viewing requires patience and luck. Plan extended stays with multiple viewing opportunities rather than hoping for success on a single night.

Pack for Extreme Cold: Bring or rent serious winter gear – thermal layers, insulated boots, warm gloves, and hand warmers. You'll be standing outside in sub-zero temperatures for hours.

Master Night Photography: Learn camera settings for low-light conditions if you want to capture images. However, remember that cameras can't match what your eyes see.

Plan Daytime Activities: Fill non-aurora hours with ice caves, glacier tours, dog sledding, or cultural experiences. Make it a complete Arctic adventure.

The Sweet Rewards

You'll master cold-weather photography and night sky observation, experience the unique culture of Arctic communities, and become someone who truly understands why people travel thousands of miles for a glimpse of green fire in the sky!

BUDGET: $3,000-$10,000 | TIME: 1-2 WEEKS | DIFFICULTY: BEGINNER

#74 Take a Guided Camping Trip

Rediscover the Great Outdoors (Without the Equipment Headaches)

Taking a guided camping trip means enjoying nature without planning stress while rediscovering your connection to the outdoors and gaining confidence through expert-led skill building. You'll discover that camping feels amazingly peaceful when experienced guides handle all the setup and safety concerns.

Getting Started

Choose Your Adventure Level: Research different camping styles – maybe luxury base camps with comfortable amenities, traditional backcountry experiences, or specialty camps focused on activities like wildlife viewing, photography, or stargazing.

Select Your Destination: Consider national parks, wilderness areas, or unique locations like desert landscapes, mountain regions, or coastal areas. Each offers different experiences and activity options.

Find Quality Outfitters: Book with established companies that provide experienced guides, quality equipment, and comprehensive support. Look for operators specializing in your age group and interests.

Assess Physical Requirements: Understand activity levels, hiking distances, and accommodation styles. Most guided trips accommodate various fitness levels but communicate your needs clearly.

Pack Appropriately: Follow provided packing lists but focus on personal comfort items.

Prepare for Simplicity: Embrace the break from technology, complex schedules, and urban conveniences. Guided camping offers rare opportunities to slow down and connect with natural rhythms.

Learn from Experts: Take advantage of guides' knowledge about local wildlife, plants, weather patterns, and outdoor skills. Ask questions and participate in educational activities.

The Sweet Rewards

You'll reconnect with the natural world in ways that feel nostalgic and exciting, learn from experienced guides who make outdoor skills seem achievable, and surprise yourself by how much you enjoy disconnecting from technology and daily routines!

BUDGET: $1,500-$5,000 | TIME: 3-10 DAYS | DIFFICULTY: BEG. TO INTERM.

#75 Stay at a Historic House in the UK

Sleep Where History Was Made (And Live Like Royalty for a Week)

Staying at a historic house in the UK means sleeping in extraordinary properties that witnessed pivotal British history, from medieval castles to Georgian estates. You'll experience how aristocracy lived while enjoying modern comforts integrated into ancient walls without compromising authentic atmosphere.

Getting Started

Choose Your Historical Period: Research different eras – maybe a Norman castle for medieval atmosphere, a Tudor manor for Renaissance charm, a Georgian country house for elegant refinement, or a Victorian mansion for industrial-age grandeur.

Select Your Experience Level: Consider castle hotels with full service, National Trust properties offering unique accommodations, or private historic homes operating as luxury B&Bs. Each provides different levels of authenticity and amenities.

Plan Extended Stays: Don't rush – historic houses deserve time to appreciate their architecture, explore grounds, and absorb their atmosphere. Consider week-long stays to truly settle in.

Pack Appropriately: Bring comfortable walking shoes for exploring, layers for variable heating, and perhaps formal wear if dining rooms maintain traditional dress codes.

Embrace the Quirks: Historic properties often feature uneven floors, low doorways, drafty corners, and plumbing that requires patience. These "inconveniences" are part of the authentic experience.

Explore the Grounds: Most historic houses feature magnificent gardens, walking paths, and outbuildings. Allow time to wander estates and understand how these properties functioned.

Connect with Local History: Visit nearby villages, churches, and museums that provide context for your historic house experience. Understanding regional history enriches your stay.

Plan Seasonal Visits: Consider how different seasons affect historic properties – cozy winter evenings by massive fireplaces, or spring gardens coming alive around ancient walls.

The Sweet Rewards

You'll literally live inside British history, experience authentic period architecture, enjoy unparalleled luxury in unique settings, and truly feel like the lord or lady of the manor!

BUDGET: $200-$1,500 PER NIGHT | TIME: 3-14 DAYS | DIFFICULTY: BEGINNER

#76 Take a Cultural Immersion Trip

Experience Authentic Culture Through Real Family Life

Taking a cultural immersion trip living with local families means choosing authentic experiences over tourist packages while sharing daily meals, participating in customs, and engaging in conversations that reveal how people actually live in ways no guidebook could show you.

Getting Started

Choose Your Destination Thoughtfully: Research countries where homestay programs are well-established and safe. Consider places with cultures genuinely different from your own – maybe rural Japan, mountain villages in Peru, or coastal towns in Portugal.

Select Reputable Programs: Work with established organizations that screen families, provide cultural orientation, and offer support during your stay. Look for programs emphasizing mutual cultural exchange rather than just accommodation.

Prepare Culturally: Learn basic language phrases, understand local customs, and research cultural norms around family life, meal times, and personal space. Respectful preparation shows genuine interest.

Plan Meaningful Duration: Stay long enough for relationships to develop – typically 1-3 weeks minimum. Shorter visits feel touristy; longer stays allow you to become part of family routines.

Bring Thoughtful Gifts: Research appropriate gifts from your home area – maybe local specialties or items representing your culture that families would genuinely appreciate.

Learn Through Living: Ask about local traditions, join cooking sessions, accompany family members to work or social events, and share your own culture and stories.

Give Back: Consider ways to support your host family or community after your return – maybe through continued correspondence, small financial support, or helping other travelers connect respectfully.

The Sweet Rewards

You'll gain authentic cultural understanding, form genuine international friendships, and return with perspectives that forever change how you see both travel and humanity!

BUDGET: $1,500-$5,000 | TIME: 1-4 WEEKS | DIFFICULTY: INTERMEDIATE

#77 Learn a New Language and Plan a Trip

Break Down Language Barriers and Open Cultural Doors

Learning a new language and planning a trip to practice it combines intellectual challenge with real-world adventure while transforming travel from surface-level tourism into profound cultural experiences. You'll discover that speaking even basic phrases opens doors to experiences that remain closed to tourists relying on translation apps.

Getting Started

Choose Your Language Strategically: Pick a language that genuinely excites you or connects to your heritage, travel plans, or personal interests. Maybe Spanish for Latin America adventures, Italian for Renaissance art appreciation, or Japanese for cultural fascination.

Mix Learning Methods: Combine apps like Duolingo or Babbel with conversation classes, online tutors, or local language exchange groups. Variety keeps learning engaging and addresses different skill areas.

Set Realistic Goals: Aim for conversational basics rather than fluency. Focus on practical phrases for travel, dining, shopping, and simple conversations that enhance cultural connections.

Practice Daily: Even 15-30 minutes daily creates steady progress. Make it routine – maybe morning coffee with vocabulary or evening podcasts in your target language.

Find Conversation Partners: Join local language meetups, hire online tutors, or connect with native speakers through language exchange apps. Real conversation builds confidence faster than solo study.

Immerse Yourself Locally: Watch movies, listen to music, read simple books, and follow social media accounts in your target language. Create a mini-immersion environment at home.

Plan Your Practice Trip: Research destinations where you can use your new skills – maybe language immersion programs, homestays, or guided tours conducted in your target language.

The Sweet Rewards

You'll exercise your brain, transform travel experiences, build connections with new communities, and become the person who can navigate foreign countries with confidence. Plus, you'll gain deep appreciation for other cultures through their languages!

BUDGET: $500-$5,000 | TIME: 30 MIN-2 HRS DAILY | DIFFICULTY: INTERM.

EDUCATIONAL OPPORTUNITIES

#78 Take a Master Class from Experts

Learn from the Experts Without Leaving Your Living Room

Taking master classes from famous experts combines unprecedented access to world-renowned teachers while learning proven techniques directly from people at the pinnacle of their fields and gaining invaluable insights you cannot find in books. You'll find that studying with legends provides not just technical knowledge but inspiration that transforms your approach to creativity.

Getting Started

Choose Your Fascinations: Browse platforms like MasterClass, CreativeLive, or The Great Courses to find subjects that genuinely excite you. Maybe cooking with Gordon Ramsay, writing with Margaret Atwood, photography with Annie Leibovitz, or chess with Garry Kasparov.

Mix High and Low Stakes: Combine practical skills you'll use (cooking, gardening, communication) with pure passion projects (filmmaking, music, creative writing). Variety keeps learning fresh and engaging.

Create Learning Schedules: Treat classes seriously by setting regular viewing times, taking notes, and completing assignments. The best master classes require active participation, not passive watching.

Practice Actively: Don't just watch – do the exercises, try the techniques, and apply lessons to your own projects. Learning happens through practice, not observation.

Join Communities: Many platforms offer discussion forums where students share work and insights. Connect with fellow learners who share your interests and enthusiasm.

Apply Lessons Broadly: Use insights from one field in another – maybe photography composition principles in painting, or negotiation techniques in community organizing.

Share Your Learning: Teach friends or family what you're discovering, start projects based on lessons, or join local groups related to your new interests.

The Sweet Rewards

You'll gain expertise from world-renowned masters without leaving your home, develop skills using techniques that have created legendary careers, challenge yourself with advanced concepts that push your abilities to new levels, and maybe find yourself pursuing passions you thought were beyond your reach!

BUDGET: $200-$1,000 | TIME: 3-10 HRS/WEEK | DIFFICULTY: BEG. TO INTERM.

#79 Audit Interesting College Courses

Return to Academia as a Student of Pure Curiosity

Auditing college courses means attending classes without pressure from grades, tests, or degree requirements that interfere with pure learning. This approach allows you to explore subjects you've always been curious about without worrying about homework, focusing instead on engaging with ideas and contributing insights from life experience.

Getting Started

Research Your Options: Contact local colleges and universities about their audit policies. Many institutions welcome older learners and offer special programs or reduced fees for seniors.

Choose Your Passion Subjects: Pick courses you've always wanted to take – maybe art history, philosophy, creative writing, astronomy, or world religions. This is your chance to explore pure curiosity.

Connect with Professors: Introduce yourself and explain your interests. Most professors love engaged older students who bring real-world perspectives to academic discussions.

Prepare Like a Student: Do the readings, participate in discussions, and engage with the material. You're not just sitting in – you're learning alongside degree-seeking students.

Build Study Habits: Create schedules for reading, note-taking, and reflection. Treat your education seriously even without grades motivating you.

Connect with Classmates: Don't be the intimidating older person in the corner. Share your perspectives, learn from younger students, and maybe become an informal mentor.

Consider Online Options: Many universities offer online courses that provide flexibility while maintaining academic rigor. Perfect for exploring subjects without commuting to campus.

The Sweet Rewards

You'll engage your mind with challenging material, interact with brilliant professors and motivated students, and gain deep knowledge in subjects you love while proving that learning never stops being exciting!

BUDGET: $100-$2,000/COURSE | TIME: 10-15 HRS/WEEK | DIFFICULTY: INTERM.

#80 Trace Your Family History

Discover the Fascinating Characters in Your Family Tree

Studying genealogy and tracing your family history combines building family trees while gaining understanding of your ancestral origins and preserving stories for future generations.

Getting Started

Interview Living Relatives: Start with the oldest family members who remember stories, names, and dates. Record conversations and ask about family legends, immigration stories, and old family photos.

Gather Physical Evidence: Collect birth certificates, marriage licenses, death certificates, military records, and immigration documents. These official papers provide the foundation for accurate research.

Choose Your Research Platform: Sign up for services like Ancestry.com, FamilySearch, or MyHeritage that provide access to historical records, census data, and DNA matching services.

Learn Research Techniques: Take online courses or join local genealogy societies to learn proper research methods, record evaluation, and source documentation. Good genealogy requires detective skills.

Take DNA Tests: Use services like AncestryDNA or 23andMe to connect with genetic relatives and verify family connections. DNA often reveals surprises and breaks through research walls.

Connect with Distant Cousins: Reach out to DNA matches and other researchers working on the same family lines. Collaboration often reveals new information and family stories.

Share Your Discoveries: Create family websites, write family histories, or present research to family reunions. Your work becomes a gift to current and future generations.

Join Communities: Connect with local genealogy groups, online forums, or ethnic heritage societies. Other researchers share tips, resources, and encouragement.

The Sweet Rewards

You'll solve family mysteries that have puzzled relatives for decades, connect with distant cousins around the world who share your bloodline and stories, experience the thrill of discovering ancestors who lived through major historical events, and create a lasting legacy that helps future generations understand their roots and identity!

BUDGET: $200-$2,000 | TIME: 5-20 HRS/WEEK | DIFFICULTY: INTERMEDIATE

#81 Become a Certified Sommelier

Turn Wine Tasting from Hobby to High Art

Learning about wine and pursuing sommelier certification combines elevated tastings while developing sophisticated sensory skills that allow you to detect subtle flavors most people cannot perceive and gaining expertise that transforms every meal into an educational opportunity to appreciate the craftsmanship behind each bottle.

Getting Started

Choose Your Certification Path: Research programs from the Court of Master Sommeliers, Wine & Spirit Education Trust (WSET), or Society of Wine Educators. Each offers different approaches and levels of study.

Start with Fundamentals: Learn about grape varieties, wine regions, production methods, and tasting techniques. Take introductory courses that cover basics before attempting advanced certifications.

Develop Your Palate: Practice systematic tasting using proper techniques. Learn to identify flavors, aromas, and structural elements. Start a tasting journal to track your progress.

Study Wine Geography: Understand how climate, soil, and tradition shape different wine regions. Learn why Champagne tastes different from Prosecco and what makes Napa special.

Join Wine Communities: Connect with local wine clubs, tasting groups, or sommelier organizations. Other wine lovers share knowledge, recommendations, and tasting opportunities.

Build Your Cellar: Start collecting wines to study and age. Understanding how wines evolve requires tasting the same wine at different stages.

Take Practice Exams: Sommelier certifications include blind tasting and written exams. Practice regularly with study groups or online resources.

Consider Specializations: Focus on specific regions, styles, or aspects of wine that particularly interest you – maybe natural wines, fortified wines, or specific countries.

The Sweet Rewards

You'll master food and wine pairing that elevates both to new heights, join an exclusive community of wine professionals, potentially start a wine collection with confidence based on knowledge, and experience wine in ways casual drinkers never achieve.

BUDGET: $1,000-$5,000 | TIME: 10-20 HRS/WEEK | DIFFICULTY: INTERM. TO ADV

#82 Visit to a Dark Sky Park

Journey to the Stars Without Leaving Earth

Taking up astronomy and visiting dark sky parks transforms casual stargazing into scientific exploration while helping you connect with cosmic wonders, understand the science behind stars and galaxies, and experience pristine night skies our ancestors took for granted before light pollution.

Getting Started

Learn the Basics: Start with astronomy books, apps like SkySafari or Star Walk, and online courses. Understand what you're seeing before investing in expensive equipment.

Start Simple: Begin with binoculars and naked-eye observations. Learn major constellations, bright planets, and seasonal sky changes. Master the basics before moving to telescopes.

Join Astronomy Groups: Connect with local astronomy clubs or societies. Experienced stargazers love sharing knowledge and often let newcomers try different telescopes.

Choose Your Equipment: When ready, invest in a quality beginner telescope. Consider refractors for planetary viewing or reflectors for deep-sky objects. Don't start too big – portability matters.

Plan Dark Sky Adventures: Research International Dark Sky Parks or reserves near you. These protected areas offer incredible night sky viewing impossible in light-polluted cities.

Learn Sky Navigation: Master using star charts, understand celestial coordinates, and practice finding objects. Apps help, but traditional navigation skills enhance the experience.

Track Celestial Events: Follow astronomical calendars for meteor showers, eclipses, planetary conjunctions, and other special events. These create memorable observing opportunities.

The Sweet Rewards

You'll witness breathtaking celestial events like meteor showers and eclipses with expert understanding, develop the ability to navigate using stars like ancient mariners, and experience profound moments of wonder that put daily concerns into cosmic perspective!

BUDGET: $200-$5,000 | TIME: 5-15 HRS/WEEK | DIFFICULTY: BEG. TO INTERM.

#83 Become a Meditation Instructor

Master the Art of Inner Peace (And Help Others Find Theirs)

Learning meditation and becoming a certified instructor involves developing personal calm while gaining expertise that transforms your relationship with stress, then sharing these practices with others searching for peace. You'll combine personal growth with meaningful service, helping people quiet their minds and develop inner resources to navigate life's difficulties.

Getting Started

Explore Different Styles: Try various approaches – mindfulness, loving-kindness, body scan, or breathing techniques. Find methods that resonate with your personality and needs.

Establish Daily Practice: Start with 5-10 minutes daily and gradually increase. Consistency matters more than duration. Use apps like Headspace or Insight Timer for initial guidance.

Take Formal Training: Enroll in teacher training programs through established organizations like Mindfulness-Based Stress Reduction (MBSR), local meditation centers, or online platforms.

Study the Science: Learn about meditation's effects on the brain, stress reduction, and physical health. Understanding research helps you teach with confidence.

Practice Teaching Early: Start sharing techniques with friends, family, or small groups. Teaching reinforces your learning while building confidence.

Pursue Certification: Complete formal programs that include practice teaching, feedback, and mentorship. Most require 200+ hours of training and personal practice.

Develop Your Style: Discover your natural teaching voice – maybe gentle and nurturing, practical and scientific, or incorporating movement and creativity.

Build Your Community: Connect with local meditation groups, wellness centers, or healthcare facilities that might welcome qualified instructors.

The Sweet Rewards

You'll develop unshakeable inner calm that carries you through life's challenges, build a fulfilling practice of guiding others toward emotional balance, potentially create meaningful income teaching skills that improve lives, and become the person who radiates peaceful presence that others seek during difficult times!

BUDGET: $500-$3,000 | TIME: 1-3 HRS DAILY | DIFFICULTY: INTERMEDIATE

#84 Get a New Degree Here or Abroad

Turn Your Intellectual Dreams into Academic Reality

Getting a new degree transforms retirement into your most intellectually exciting chapter while pursuing knowledge purely for curiosity rather than career advancement. This journey allows you to explore subjects you've always been passionate about, discovering that returning to education brings unique advantages including better appreciation for learning.

Getting Started

Choose Your Passion Subject: Pick fields that genuinely excite you – maybe art history, environmental science, psychology, literature, or archaeology. This is your chance to study what you've always wondered about.

Research University Options: Consider local institutions for convenience, or explore international programs for cultural immersion. Many universities welcome mature students and offer flexible schedules.

Understand Admission Requirements: Most schools have pathways for non-traditional students. Your life experience often counts more than old transcripts for mature applicants.

Plan Your Timeline: Decide between full-time intensive study or part-time programs that allow travel. Many universities offer evening or weekend classes.

Consider International Options: Study abroad programs designed for seniors offer incredible cultural experiences. Imagine earning a degree in Italian Renaissance art while living in Florence!

Explore Degree Types: Choose from bachelor's degrees in new fields, master's programs, or doctoral studies. Some schools offer interdisciplinary programs perfect for broad interests.

Budget Realistically: Factor in tuition, books, travel, and living expenses. Many universities offer senior discounts that reduce costs.

Join Student Life: Participate in clubs, events, and study groups. Your perspectives enrich campus communities while building lasting friendships.

The Sweet Rewards

You'll gain credentials that establish your expertise in areas you care about, experience the satisfaction of mastering challenging material without career pressure, and join the ranks of lifelong learners who understand that education is a gift you give yourself rather than just a means to an end!

BUDGET: $5,000-$50,000+ | TIME: 2-6 YEARS | DIFFICULTY: ADVANCED

#85 Embrace Sustainable Living

Turn Your Home into a Self-Sustaining Paradise

Learning sustainable living and going off-grid transforms your approach to resource consumption while mastering energy systems, water management, and waste reduction that create self-sufficient systems. You'll develop expertise in renewable energy that allows comfortable living while being completely independent from utility companies and conventional grid systems.

Getting Started

Study Energy Systems: Learn about solar panels, wind turbines, battery storage, and backup generators. Understanding how these systems work together is crucial for reliable off-grid power.

Assess Your Property: Evaluate sun exposure, wind patterns, water sources, and soil conditions. Good off-grid planning starts with understanding your land's natural resources.

Start Small: Begin with partial systems like solar garden lights or backup power for essential appliances. Gradually expand as you gain experience and confidence.

Master Water Management: Learn about well drilling, rainwater collection, greywater systems, and water purification. Clean water is essential for comfortable off-grid living.

Design Waste Systems: Study composting toilets, septic systems, and waste reduction strategies. Effective waste management is crucial when you can't rely on municipal services.

Learn Food Production: Develop gardening skills, food preservation techniques, and livestock management if appropriate. Food security enhances off-grid independence.

Build Essential Skills: Master basic electrical work, plumbing, and equipment maintenance. Off-grid living requires hands-on problem-solving abilities.

Connect with Communities: Join off-grid forums, visit demonstration sites, and learn from experienced practitioners. The off-grid community is generous with knowledge.

The Sweet Rewards

You'll become a living example of environmental stewardship that inspires others, gain expertise in sustainable technologies that position you as a local resource, and enjoy peace of mind knowing you can thrive regardless of external economic or infrastructure challenges!

BUDGET: $10,000-$100,000+ | TIME: 20-40 HRS/WEEK | DIFFICULTY: ADV.

#86 Become a Certified Life Coach

Turn Your Life Lessons into Professional Expertise That Changes Lives

Becoming a certified life coach or counselor means developing professional skills to guide others through life transitions and challenges. It's about combining your life experience with proven techniques to make meaningful differences when people need guidance most.

Getting Started

Choose Your Path: Decide between life coaching (focuses on goals and future) or counseling (addresses past issues and mental health). Each requires different training and serves different client needs.

Research Certification Programs: Look for accredited programs through organizations like the International Coach Federation (ICF) for coaching or state-licensed programs for counseling. Quality training is essential.

Understand Training Requirements: Life coaching certification typically requires 60-125 hours of training, while counseling demands 500+ hours plus supervised practice. Plan accordingly for your chosen path.

Develop Core Skills: Learn active listening, powerful questioning, goal setting, and ethical boundaries. These foundational skills apply to both coaching and counseling approaches.

Find Your Specialization: Consider focusing on specific areas like career transitions, retirement planning, relationship coaching, or grief counseling based on your interests and experience.

Maintain Continuing Education: Both fields require ongoing learning to maintain certifications. Attend workshops, conferences, and advanced training programs regularly.

Consider Your Setting: Decide whether to work independently, join existing practices, partner with healthcare providers, or offer services through community organizations.

The Sweet Rewards

You'll make meaningful differences in people's lives, use your wisdom professionally, potentially earn good income, and find deep satisfaction helping others achieve their goals and overcome challenges!

BUDGET: $2,000-$15,000 | TIME: 10-25 HRS/WK | DIFFICULTY: INTERM. TO ADV.

ATHLETIC ENDEAVORS

#87 Complete a Competitive Event

Transform Your Fitness Journey into Personal Achievement

Training for and completing a competitive event means choosing a challenging goal and systematically preparing through dedicated training. This commitment teaches valuable lessons about goal-setting and perseverance while building fitness and confidence that extends beyond the specific sport you choose.

Getting Started

Choose Your Challenge: Pick an event that excites and slightly intimidates you – maybe a local 5K, charity bike ride, swimming meet, or even a triathlon. Consider your current fitness level and interests.

Assess Your Starting Point: Get medical clearance from your doctor and honestly evaluate your current fitness. This becomes your baseline for measuring progress.

Create a Training Plan: Develop a systematic approach with gradual progression over 12-16 weeks. Include cardio, strength training, flexibility work, and rest days for recovery.

Find Your Support System: Join training groups, hire a coach, or connect with other participants. Having accountability partners makes training more enjoyable and effective.

Invest in Proper Equipment: Get quality shoes, appropriate clothing, and any sport-specific gear. Proper equipment prevents injuries and enhances performance.

Track Your Progress: Keep training logs, monitor improvements, and celebrate milestones. Seeing progress motivates continued effort during challenging periods.

Practice Race Conditions: Train in similar weather, terrain, and timing as your event. Practice nutrition, hydration, and equipment strategies during training.

Build Mental Toughness: Prepare for discomfort, setbacks, and race-day nerves. Mental preparation is as important as physical training.

Plan Recovery: Include rest days, proper nutrition, and sleep in your training. Recovery is when your body actually gets stronger.

The Sweet Rewards

You'll achieve fitness levels you thought were impossible, gain confidence in your capabilities, inspire others, and become the person whose determination proves that age truly is just a number!

BUDGET: $200-$2,000 | TIME: 5-10 HRS/WEEK | DIFFICULTY: INTERMEDIATE

#88 Learn Martial Arts (Tai Chi, Aikido)

Master Ancient Arts That Build Strength, Balance, and Inner Peace

Learning martial arts means mastering ancient techniques that combine physical conditioning, mental discipline, and spiritual development. Whether you choose Tai Chi, Karate, or Aikido, the practice is about becoming stronger in body and mind while learning self-defense skills and valuable lessons about patience and self-control.

Getting Started

Choose Your Style: Research different martial arts – Tai Chi for gentle, meditative movement; Karate for traditional strikes and discipline; Aikido for defensive techniques using opponent's energy; or Judo for throws and grappling.

Find Quality Instruction: Look for schools that welcome adult beginners and emphasize safety, proper technique, and gradual progression.

Start Slowly: Begin with basic movements, stances, and breathing techniques. Focus on form and understanding rather than speed or power initially.

Embrace the Philosophy: Learn about the mental and spiritual aspects of your chosen art. Most martial arts emphasize respect, discipline, and personal growth beyond physical techniques.

Practice Regularly: Consistency matters more than intensity. Even 20-30 minutes of daily practice builds muscle memory and improves technique significantly.

Focus on Balance and Flexibility: Many martial arts improve coordination, balance, and joint mobility – benefits that become increasingly valuable with age.

Learn from Everyone: Train with students of all ages and skill levels. Younger students teach energy and enthusiasm; experienced practitioners share wisdom and technique.

Set Personal Goals: Work toward belt progressions or skill milestones that challenge you appropriately. Progress may be slower than younger students, but it's equally meaningful.

The Sweet Rewards

You'll improve strength, balance, and flexibility while learning practical self-defense skills, developing mental discipline, and joining a supportive community that values respect and personal growth!

BUDGET: $100-$200 MONTHLY | TIME: 3-6 HRS/WK | DIFFICULTY: BEGINNER

#89 Become a Certified Yoga Instructor

Turn Your Practice into a Way to Help Others Find Balance

Becoming a certified yoga instructor means mastering an ancient practice that combines physical postures, breathing techniques, and mindfulness while developing skills to guide others safely on their wellness journeys. This certification deepens your own practice while teaching you to adapt poses for different abilities.

Getting Started

Develop Your Personal Practice: Establish a regular yoga routine before teaching others. Take classes, work with experienced instructors, and explore different styles like Hatha, Vinyasa, or Restorative yoga.

Choose Your Training Program: Research 200-hour teacher training programs through Yoga Alliance certified schools. Look for programs that emphasize anatomy, philosophy, and teaching methodology.

Study Yoga Philosophy: Learn about yoga's ancient roots, ethical principles, and spiritual aspects. Understanding philosophy helps you teach with depth and authenticity.

Master Anatomy and Safety: Study how the body moves, common injuries, and modifications for different abilities. Safe teaching protects students and builds confidence.

Practice Teaching: Start with friends, family, or volunteer opportunities. Teaching builds confidence while helping you develop your unique style and voice.

Learn Modifications: Study how to adapt poses for different ages, injuries, and flexibility levels. Your classes should welcome everyone, regardless of physical limitations.

Find Your Teaching Style: Discover whether you prefer gentle, restorative classes or more dynamic sessions, and let your authentic style shine through.

Build Your Classes: Start teaching at community centers, senior centers, or studios. Many places welcome qualified instructors who understand mature students' needs.

Continue Learning: Pursue advanced training, workshops, and continuing education. The best yoga teachers remain lifelong students.

The Sweet Rewards

You'll deepen your own practice, help others improve their health and well-being, potentially earn income sharing something you love, and become a source of calm in a chaotic world!

BUDGET: $2,000-$5,000 | TIME: 10-20 HRS/WEEK | DIFFICULTY: INTERM.

#90 Learn to Dance (Ballroom, Salsa, Swing)

Master the Art of Moving to Music with Confidence and Style

Learning to dance means mastering rhythmic movement with a partner while developing coordination and timing that transforms music into shared expression. This practice teaches you to listen to music deeply, trust your partner, and express emotions through movement while building confidence.

Getting Started

Choose Your Style: Research different dance forms – ballroom for elegance and tradition, salsa for passion and energy, swing for fun and athleticism, or tango for drama and intensity. Each offers unique rewards and challenges.

Find Quality Instruction: Look for studios that specialize in social dancing and welcome beginners. Group classes provide community, while private lessons offer personalized attention.

Start with Basics: Focus on fundamental steps, posture, and rhythm before attempting complex moves. Good foundation skills make everything else easier and more enjoyable.

Practice Patience: Dancing requires coordination between partners, which takes time to develop. Expect initial awkwardness – everyone goes through this learning phase.

Attend Social Dances: Visit dance nights, practice parties, or social events where you can practice with different partners. Real dancing happens outside of lessons.

Invest in Proper Shoes: Dance shoes with suede soles make movement easier and safer. Proper footwear prevents injuries and enhances performance.

Learn Partner Etiquette: Understand dance floor courtesy, how to ask for dances respectfully, and social customs that make events enjoyable for everyone.

Build Confidence Gradually: Start with easier dances and simpler steps. As skills improve, challenge yourself with more complex rhythms and patterns.

Join the Community: Participate in dance events, competitions, or themed parties. The dance community is social and welcoming to enthusiastic learners.

The Sweet Rewards

You'll improve coordination and fitness, express creativity through movement, build social connections, and discover the pure joy of moving to music with others!

BUDGET: $300-$2,000 | TIME: 4-8 HRS/WEEK | DIFFICULTY: BEG. TO INTERM.

#91 Train for a Long-Distance Hike or Walk

Build Hiking Endurance That Opens Up New Adventure Possibilities

Training for a long-distance hike means systematically building endurance, strength, and mental resilience through progressive conditioning that prepares your body for challenging trails. This journey teaches valuable lessons about perseverance and builds fitness, mental toughness, and confidence that extends beyond the specific trail you choose.

Getting Started

Choose Your Challenge: Pick a specific goal – maybe a 50-mile charity walk, section hiking on famous trails, or multi-day wilderness adventures. Having a concrete target motivates consistent training.

Assess Your Starting Point: Get medical clearance and honestly evaluate current fitness levels. Start where you are, not where you think you should be.

Build Base Mileage: Begin with comfortable distances and gradually increase weekly mileage by 10%. Consistency matters more than speed initially.

Strengthen Supporting Muscles: Include exercises for core stability, hip strength, and ankle mobility. Strong supporting muscles prevent overuse injuries during long hikes.

Test Your Gear: Use training hikes to break in boots, test clothing systems, and practice with navigation tools. Discover what works before your big adventure.

Train on Similar Terrain: If your goal involves hills, train on hills. If it's rocky trails, find similar surfaces. Specificity in training pays off on event day.

Build Mental Toughness: Practice hiking when tired, in poor weather, or when motivation is low. Mental preparation is crucial for long-distance success.

Plan Recovery: Include rest days, proper nutrition, and sleep in your training. Recovery is when your body adapts and gets stronger.

Join Training Groups: Connect with other long-distance hikers for motivation, safety, and shared wisdom. Training partners make difficult days more enjoyable.

The Sweet Rewards

You'll achieve fitness levels you thought were impossible, gain confidence in your physical capabilities, enjoy incredible natural scenery, and become the person whose hiking stories inspire others to push their boundaries!

BUDGET: $300-$2,000 | TIME: 6-15 HRS/WEEK | DIFFICULTY: INTERM. TO ADV.

#92 Do a Multi-Day Cycling Tour

Rediscover the Joy of Two Wheels (And See the World at the Perfect Pace)

Taking up cycling and doing a multi-day bike tour means combining the joy of riding with travel adventure while discovering that bicycles can carry you farther than imagined, providing an eco-friendly way to explore at the perfect pace for experiencing landscapes and communities.

Getting Started

Choose the Right Bike: Consider touring bikes, hybrid bikes, or e-bikes depending on your fitness level and tour ambitions. Visit bike shops to test different styles and get proper fitting.

Build Your Fitness: Start with short local rides and gradually increase distance and duration. Build base fitness before attempting multi-day tours.

Learn Basic Maintenance: Master tire changes, chain lubrication, and basic adjustments. Mechanical skills provide confidence and independence on longer tours.

Plan Your First Tour: Start with supported tours where luggage is transported, or choose well-established routes with frequent lodging options. Build experience before attempting self-supported adventures.

Invest in Proper Gear: Quality bike shorts, helmets, and touring equipment make long days in the saddle comfortable. Don't skimp on items that affect comfort and safety.

Practice Loaded Riding: If planning self-supported tours, practice riding with panniers and gear. Loaded bikes handle differently than unloaded ones.

Choose Scenic Routes: Research bike-friendly routes, rail-trails, or dedicated cycling paths. Beautiful scenery makes miles pass more enjoyably.

Plan Rest and Recovery: Include rest days, comfortable accommodations, and massage into tour plans. Enjoyment matters more than daily mileage goals.

The Sweet Rewards

You'll develop incredible fitness, see landscapes from unique perspectives, meet fellow cycling enthusiasts, and become the person whose vacation stories include pedaling through amazing destinations under your own power!

BUDGET: $1,000-$8,000+ | TIME: 8-20 HRS/WEEK | DIFFICULTY: INTERMEDIATE

#93 Try Out a New Sport

Try Something New and Unlock Abilities You Didn't Know You Had

Trying out a new sport means stepping outside your comfort zone to explore activities you've never attempted while discovering that age is often just a mental barrier when it comes to athletic adventure. You'll discover that trying new sports builds confidence, improves coordination, and often reveals hidden talents.

Getting Started

Explore Your Options: Research sports that appeal to you – maybe tennis, pickleball, swimming, badminton, bowling, golf, or disc golf. Consider both individual and team sports.

Start with Lessons: Take beginner classes or hire instructors who work with adult learners. Proper instruction prevents bad habits and builds confidence safely.

Try Before You Buy: Rent or borrow equipment initially to test your interest level. Many facilities provide equipment for beginners.

Find Beginner-Friendly Groups: Look for clubs or groups specifically for newcomers. Avoid highly competitive environments while learning.

Focus on Fundamentals: Master basic skills before attempting advanced techniques. Good foundations make everything else more enjoyable.

Set Realistic Goals: Aim for personal improvement rather than comparing yourself to others. Celebrate small victories and steady progress.

Embrace the Learning Process: Expect mistakes and awkward moments – they're part of the fun! Maintain a sense of humor about your learning journey.

Consider Physical Demands: Choose sports appropriate for your fitness level. Adapt rules or equipment as needed for comfort and safety.

Make It Social: Join clubs, attend group activities, or find playing partners. The social aspect often becomes as valuable as the physical activity.

Listen to Your Body: Pay attention to how activities feel and adjust intensity accordingly. Smart athletes prevent injuries through self-awareness.

The Sweet Rewards

You'll discover new physical abilities, meet like-minded people, improve fitness and coordination, and maybe find a lifelong passion that keeps you active!

BUDGET: $100-$1,000 | TIME: 3-8 HRS/WEEK | DIFFICULTY: BEG. TO INTERM.

#94 Start a Walking or Hiking Club

Create the Walking Group That Makes Exercise Social and Fun

Starting a walking or hiking club means creating a supportive group where people of similar fitness levels can explore local trails together while building friendships and making outdoor activity social, safe, and accessible. This effort creates accountability for regular exercise while providing safety from exploring unfamiliar trails with knowledgeable companions. You'll discover that leading a walking group creates lasting friendships and establishes regular activities that keep everyone active and connected to nature.

Getting Started

Define Your Club's Focus: Decide between casual neighborhood walks, nature trail hikes, or mixed activities. Consider your target audience's fitness levels and interests.

Find Your Founding Members: Start with friends, neighbors, or acquaintances who enjoy walking. Post on community boards or social media to attract like-minded people.

Choose Meeting Logistics: Establish regular meeting times, locations, and communication methods. Consistency helps people plan and builds commitment to the group.

Scout Safe Routes: Research local trails, parks, and walking paths. Consider distance, difficulty, parking, and restroom availability when planning routes.

Plan for All Weather: Develop alternatives for rainy days – maybe indoor venues like malls or covered walkways. Keep the group active year-round.

Create Safety Protocols: Establish buddy systems, emergency contact procedures, and guidelines for different fitness levels. Safety builds confidence and participation.

Make It Social: Plan post-walk coffee stops, seasonal celebrations, or special destination hikes. Social connections keep people engaged beyond just exercise.

Welcome Newcomers: Create welcoming environments for new members with different experience levels. Growth strengthens the community.

Track Your Adventures: Keep logs of places visited, distances covered, and group milestones. Celebrating achievements motivates continued participation.

The Sweet Rewards

You'll build lasting friendships, discover beautiful local areas, improve everyone's fitness, and become the community leader who gets people outdoors and connected!

BUDGET: $100-$500 | TIME: 3-6 HRS/WEEK | DIFFICULTY: BEGINNER

FAMILY PROJECTS

#95 Create a Detailed Family Cookbook

Turn Family Food Stories into Written History

Creating a detailed family cookbook with stories means collecting beloved recipes while documenting the family history and traditions that make each dish special to your heritage. This project transforms recipe collection into family storytelling as you interview relatives and document the stories behind holiday traditions that shaped your family's culinary identity.

Getting Started

Gather Family Recipes: Contact relatives to collect handwritten recipe cards, family favorites, and holiday traditions. Many families have treasured recipes that exist only in someone's memory.

Conduct Recipe Interviews: Talk to family cooks about techniques, ingredient substitutions, and cooking stories. Ask about special occasions when dishes were served and family reactions.

Test and Document: Cook each recipe carefully, noting exact measurements, cooking times, and any missing steps. Many family recipes assume knowledge that needs clarification.

Collect Stories: Record the history behind each dish – who created it, when it was served, family memories associated with it, and any funny cooking disasters.

Organize by Themes: Structure your cookbook by categories, seasons, or family branches. Include photos of the original cooks, family gatherings, and finished dishes.

Add Family Context: Include family trees, immigration stories, regional influences, and how recipes evolved over generations.

Design for Sharing: Create multiple copies for family members, consider professional printing, or develop digital versions that can be easily shared and updated.

Plan Future Updates: Leave space for new recipes and stories as the family grows and traditions evolve.

The Sweet Rewards

You'll preserve irreplaceable family culinary heritage, create meaningful gifts for relatives, strengthen family connections, and become the keeper of traditions that might otherwise disappear!

BUDGET: $200-$1,500 | TIME: 8-15 HRS/WEEK | DIFFICULTY: INTERMEDIATE

#96 Build a Tiny House for Grandchildren

Build the Special Space That Makes Your House the Best Destination

Building a tiny house for visiting grandchildren means creating a magical space designed specifically for young visitors while maintaining the balance of independence and proximity. This construction project brings generations together in planning and building activities that teach skills and strengthen family bonds.

Getting Started

Plan with Kids in Mind: Design for safety, fun, and functionality. Include built-in storage, child-sized features, and spaces for both sleeping and playing. Let grandchildren help with planning.

Choose Your Approach: Decide between hiring contractors, doing it yourself, or a hybrid approach. Consider your skills, timeline, and local building codes.

Research Local Regulations: Check zoning laws, building permits, and HOA restrictions. Some areas have specific rules about accessory dwelling units or tiny houses.

Design for Flexibility: Create spaces that work for different ages and group sizes. Include features like fold-out beds, convertible furniture, or modular components.

Include Learning Opportunities: Let grandchildren participate in age-appropriate construction tasks. Building together teaches skills while creating shared memories.

Focus on Special Features: Add elements that make it truly special – maybe a reading nook, art station, or outdoor deck. These details create the magic.

Plan Utilities: Consider electrical, plumbing, and heating needs. Even basic utilities make the space more comfortable and usable year-round.

Create House Rules: Establish guidelines that make the space feel special but safe. Let grandchildren help create their own "house rules."

Document the Process: Take photos throughout construction and create a scrapbook about building their special house together.

The Sweet Rewards

You'll create a magical space that draws grandchildren for visits, build lasting memories through shared construction, potentially add property value, and become the grandparent whose house is every child's favorite destination!

BUDGET: $5,000-$50,000 | TIME: 20-40 HRS/WEEK | DIFFICULTY: ADVANCED

#97 Create a Family Documentary

Create the Documentary That Keeps Family Stories Alive

Creating a family documentary with interviews means professionally capturing your family's history through recorded conversations and archival photos that transform ordinary memories into compelling narratives honoring your heritage. This filmmaking project allows you to guide family members through conversations about their lives while learning video techniques that transform footage into polished documentaries.

Getting Started

Plan Your Story: Decide on focus – maybe family immigration stories, wartime experiences, business history, or multi-generational perspectives on major events. Having direction guides your interviews.

Gather Equipment: Use smartphones, basic cameras, or borrowed equipment initially. Good audio matters more than perfect video – invest in external microphones for clear sound.

Research Family History: Prepare by learning basic family timelines, reviewing old photos, and understanding historical context. Background knowledge helps you ask better questions.

Schedule Interviews: Start with oldest relatives first, allowing generous time for conversations. Create comfortable settings where people feel relaxed sharing memories.

Ask Open Questions: Use prompts like "Tell me about your childhood" rather than yes/no questions. Let conversations flow naturally while gently guiding toward important topics.

Collect Supporting Materials: Gather old photos, documents, letters, and artifacts to include. These visual elements enhance storytelling and provide historical context.

Learn Basic Editing: Use simple software like iMovie or free alternatives. Focus on clear storytelling rather than fancy effects.

Plan Your Premiere: Organize family screenings to share completed documentary. Make it a celebration of family history and shared memories.

The Sweet Rewards

You'll preserve irreplaceable family stories, strengthen connections between generations, create lasting legacies for future family members, and become the family historian whose work connects everyone to their roots!

BUDGET: $200-$2,000 | TIME: 15-30 HRS/WEEK | DIFFICULTY: INTERMEDIATE

#98 Start a Family Charitable Fund

Build the Charitable Foundation That Reflects Your Family's Values

Starting a family foundation or charitable fund means establishing a formal structure for strategic giving that can involve children, grandchildren, and future generations in meaningful philanthropic decisions while creating a lasting legacy of generosity and social responsibility. It's about transforming casual charity into purposeful philanthropy with clear missions and measurable impact that brings multiple generations together around shared values and community service. This endeavor teaches younger family members about social responsibility while providing opportunities to research worthy causes and witness how contributions improve lives and strengthen communities.

Getting Started

Define Your Mission: Identify causes that genuinely matter to your family – maybe education, environmental conservation, healthcare, or local community development. Focus creates more impact than scattered giving.

Choose Your Structure: Research donor-advised funds (easier, $5,000+ minimums), private foundations (more control, $250,000+ minimums), or charitable trusts. Each has different tax benefits and complexity levels.

Involve Family Members: Create opportunities for children and grandchildren to participate in grant decisions, site visits, and cause research. Shared philanthropy builds family bonds and teaches values.

Research Effective Organizations: Learn to evaluate nonprofits through Charity Navigator or GuideStar. Focus on organizations with proven impact, good financial management, and aligned missions.

Plan Strategic Giving: Develop multi-year funding strategies rather than random donations. Consider capacity building or funding specific programs for greater impact.

Visit Grant Recipients: Schedule site visits to see your donations at work. Meeting beneficiaries makes giving more meaningful and effective.

The Sweet Rewards

You'll create a lasting family legacy, make meaningful differences in causes you care about, engage multiple generations in philanthropy, and become the family leader who turned resources into positive change!

BUDGET: $5,000-$500,000+ | TIME: 8-20 HRS/WEEK | DIFFICULTY: INTERMEDIATE

#99 Create Time Capsules for the Future

Send Messages to the Future That Will Fascinate Your Descendants

Creating time capsules for future generations means thoughtfully preserving artifacts, documents, and memories from today's world through careful curation for discovery years or decades in the future, when current events have become historical curiosities. It's about giving your descendants a fascinating window into how you lived, what you valued, and what the world was like during your time when current technologies and cultural trends were shaping daily life.

Getting Started

Choose Your Timeline: Decide whether to create capsules for 10, 25, or 50+ years in the future. Different timeframes require different preservation methods and content strategies.

Select Meaningful Contents: Include family photos, letters to descendants, current newspapers, technological items, popular culture artifacts, and personal mementos that represent your era and family values.

Write Personal Letters: Craft messages to specific family members or future generations explaining your world, sharing wisdom, and expressing hopes for their future.

Document Daily Life: Include items that show how you lived – receipts, menus, catalogs, or small household objects that will seem quaint to future generations.

Choose Preservation Methods: Research proper storage containers, moisture protection, and preservation techniques.

Pick Strategic Locations: Decide whether to bury capsules, store them in safe deposit boxes, or entrust them to institutions. Include detailed maps and instructions for future discovery.

Create Opening Instructions: Write clear directions about when and how capsules should be opened, along with explanations of contents and their significance.

Involve Family Members: Let children and grandchildren contribute items or letters, creating shared investment in future discoveries.

The Sweet Rewards

You'll create magical surprises for future family members, preserve important historical moments, potentially provide valuable historical artifacts, and become the ancestor whose thoughtful gifts connect generations across time!

BUDGET: $100-$1,000 | TIME: 5-15 HRS/WEEK | DIFFICULTY: BEGINNER

#100 Build an Epic Backyard Playground

Create the Ultimate Outdoor Fun Zone That Kids Can't Resist

Building an elaborate backyard playground means creating a comprehensive adventure area with diverse climbing structures and imaginative play spaces designed to engage children through thoughtful design that encourages active play. This project allows you to design custom features while creating a destination that draws neighborhood children and becomes the gathering place where friendships form.

Getting Started

Design with Safety First: Research playground safety standards, proper spacing, and age-appropriate equipment. Include soft landing surfaces, secure anchoring, and clear sight lines for supervision.

Create Multiple Zones: Plan areas for different activities – maybe climbing walls, zip lines, sand play, water features, obstacle courses, and quiet reading nooks. Variety keeps children engaged longer.

Include Natural Elements: Incorporate trees, boulders, gardens, and natural materials. Kids love exploring "wild" spaces alongside structured play equipment.

Plan for All Ages: Design features for toddlers through teenagers. Consider adjustable elements, progressive challenges, and spaces where different ages can play together safely.

Add Unique Features: Include exciting elements like rope bridges, spiral slides, tire swings, or even a small zip line. Special features make your playground legendary.

Consider Year-Round Use: Add covered areas, lighting, and weather-resistant materials. Great playgrounds work in multiple seasons and conditions.

Build Gradually: Start with core structures and add features over time. This spreads costs and lets you refine designs based on how children actually use the space.

Involve Future Users: Let children help with planning and age-appropriate construction tasks. Their input creates better designs and shared ownership.

The Sweet Rewards

You'll create magical childhood experiences, encourage healthy outdoor activity, become the neighborhood's favorite destination, and build lasting memories for multiple generations of children!

BUDGET: $5,000–$50,000 | TIME: 20-40 HRS/WEEK | DIFFICULTY: ADVANCED

#101 Start a Multi-Generational Business

Build the Legacy Business That Brings Generations Together

Starting a multi-generational business means creating an enterprise that leverages different generations' unique strengths while building something meaningful that can be passed down through family lines. It's about combining your experience, relationships, and resources with your children's fresh perspectives and technological skills to create a venture benefiting from both seasoned expertise and youthful enthusiasm.

Getting Started

Identify Shared Passions: Find business ideas that genuinely excite multiple generations – maybe sustainable farming, artisan crafts, technology services, or community-focused retail. Shared enthusiasm drives success.

Leverage Generational Strengths: Use your experience for strategy and relationships, middle generations for operations and management, and younger members for technology and marketing innovation.

Define Roles Clearly: Establish who handles what aspects of the business to prevent conflicts. Create clear job descriptions, decision-making authority, and accountability structures.

Start with Pilot Projects: Test business concepts with small investments before committing major resources. Use pilots to refine family dynamics and business processes.

Plan Succession Early: Design the business for eventual transition to younger generations. Include mentorship programs, gradual responsibility shifts, and clear ownership plans.

Choose the Right Structure: Consider family limited partnerships, LLCs, or corporations that provide flexibility for multiple owners and clear governance structures.

Build on Local Connections: Use your community relationships and reputation to launch the business while teaching younger generations about networking and customer service.

The Sweet Rewards

You'll create a lasting family legacy, teach entrepreneurship to younger generations, build stronger family bonds through shared purpose, and maybe launch the next great family business dynasty!

BUDGET: $10,000-$500,000+ | TIME: 20-40 HRS/WEEK | DIFFICULTY: ADVANCED

www.ingramcontent.com/pod-product-compliance
Lightning Source LLC
Chambersburg PA
CBHW040009080526
44586CB00028B/2938